Praise For

Mindful Loving: A Guide to Loving with Passion and Purpose

A must read! *Mindful Loving: A Guide to Loving with Passion and Purpose* is an impressive book filled with real life examples and a tool box packed with practical tips that can immediately be put into use.

This powerful book is for anyone interested in improving themselves and their love relationships. As a bonus, many of the tips can be used to improve relationships and communication in business, at work, with adult siblings, and in everyday life. Concise and content-rich, each tip stands on its own. Taking the time to implement these simple and profound tips is a step along the path to purposeful and intentional Mindful Loving!

Jeanne Sharbuno, Certified Professional Coach. She is the author of *52 Ways to Live Success From the Inside Out!*

Todd and Baysinger remind us that we often think of intimate relationships as "hard work." In this book they show us in clear and practical ways how to "work smart" rather than just "work hard" in maintaining those key life connections. This jargon-free life manual should find a place on every couple's bookshelf."

Paul Lombardo, J.D., Ph.D., Professor of Law at Georgia State University, College of Law. He is the author of *Three Generations, No Imbeciles: Eugenics, the Supreme Court and* Buck v. Bell *and A Century of Eugenics in America: From the Indiana Experiment to the Human Genome Era.*

Mindful Loving: A Guide to Loving with Passion and Purpose is beautifully practical! Learn to apply the concept of mindfulness to grow a strong, resilient, rewarding relationship while gaining an understanding of the transitions of an evolving relationship. Use the "Practical Tools" as an easily accessible go-to source for approaching communication challenges of everyday life."

Christa Rice, M.Ed., CMHC, Therapist and Shamanic Energy Healer.

This is a well-organized and conceived work that is of great value to all couples interested in enhancing and protecting the quality of their relationships.

Donald E. Rice, MD, Consultation-Liaison Psychiatry, Providence Regional Medical Center Everett, WA.

Time to welcome a new perspective on relationships as Kathleen and Diana lead us into the world of Mindful Loving. I am confident couples will discover practical tools and ideas to deepen their intimacy as they are guided through a process to increase their awareness of how to better love one another.

Marcus R. Earle, Ph.D., LMFT, Clinical Director, Psychological Counseling Services, Scottsdale, Arizona. He is the co-author of *Sex Addiction: Case Studies and Management.*

Mindful Loving

A Guide to Loving with Passion and Purpose

Kathleen Todd, MSW and Diana Baysinger, MC

BALBOA.
PRESS

A DIVISION OF HAY HOUSE

Balboa Press books may be ordered through booksellers or by contacting:

Balboa Press
A Division of Hay House
1663 Liberty Drive
Bloomington, IN 47403
www.balboapress.com
1 (877) 407-4847

Because of the dynamic nature of the Internet, any web addresses or links contained in this book may have changed since publication and may no longer be valid. The views expressed in this work are solely those of the author and do not necessarily reflect the views of the publisher, and the publisher hereby disclaims any responsibility for them.

The author of this book does not dispense medical advice or prescribe the use of any technique as a form of treatment for physical, emotional, or medical problems without the advice of a physician, either directly or indirectly. The intent of the author is only to offer information of a general nature to help you in your quest for emotional and spiritual well-being. In the event you use any of the information in this book for yourself, which is your constitutional right, the author and the publisher assume no responsibility for your actions.

Print information available on the last page.

ISBN: 978-1-9822-2651-0 (sc)
ISBN: 978-1-9822-2653-4 (hc)
ISBN: 978-1-9822-2652-7 (e)

Library of Congress Control Number: 2019904565

Balboa Press rev. date: 05/13/2019

Contents

Acknowledgments

This book is a product of our combined efforts to teach and share our beliefs about how to create and grow a Mindful Loving Relationship with Passion and Purpose.

Over the years, we collected an abundance of life lessons, skills and information that have contributed to the content of *Mindful Loving: A Guide to Loving with Passion and Purpose.* These lessons, skills and information have come from both our work with clients and from our own personal discoveries and desires for life and relationship enrichment.

We are grateful for the many people who have influenced us in our professional and personal lives.

We appreciate and acknowledge all our teachers, trainers and experts who contributed to the general knowledge base and practice of psychotherapy, marriage and family therapy, sex therapy, and coaching.

We thank all our professional colleagues who have supported us and our work. Many of you encouraged us and contributed your wisdom to the evolution of our work.

A special thanks to all our clients who shared their struggles, successes, and their healing journeys with us. Psychotherapy is an intimate and unique experience for each client. This book is a synthesis of our clients' experiences and the lessons they learned during therapy. These lessons and practices are applicable and beneficial to all relationships.

We are deeply indebted to our editors who gave their time and critiques reading and editing the manuscript. Our many thanks go to Lina Alvarez, Andy Baysinger, Tyler Baysinger, Marcus Earle, Paul Lombardo, Judy Pickens, Susan Price, Donald Rice, Christa Rice, Jeanne Sharbuno, Jason Todd, and Karen Williams.

We thank the artists for their inspiration and creativity in the design of the book cover and photographs. Tommy Binkley, Jan Hayden, Susan Price, Bobbi Seiger, Adam Slaton, and Brooklyn Slaton.

Most importantly, we wish to thank our family and friends who encouraged us throughout this writing journey. Thank you for your ideas, continued interest in our progress. Our conversations about Mindful Loving have added value to the content of this book.

We are deeply grateful for the most significant contribution which has been the experience and the lessons we have learned from you and our Mindful Loving relationships with you.

Introduction

Welcome to *Mindful Loving: A Guide to Loving with Passion and Purpose.* This is a gift to you inspired by our work with thousands of couples over the past thirty years. Through our work in marriage and family therapy, sex therapy and relationship coaching, we have learned how important it is to navigate through the challenges, celebrations, and cycles of loving. It has been our privilege to partner with clients who have shared vulnerable and intimate details of their lives and love relationships.

We have worked with individuals and couples who have presented with distress, pain, and despair. Through their commitment to heal, they developed the necessary skills and practices that transformed their relationships into Mindful Loving relationships. We have been inspired by the resilience of couples who have moved from pain to loving with passion and purpose.

Mindful Loving is a conscious decision to love with intention and attention. It involves being present, thoughtful, and open to the experience of loving and being loved. Mindful Loving is dynamic and ever-changing. Throughout the course of our love relationships, there are natural ongoing cycles of connection and engagement coupled with cycles of disconnection and withdrawal. Understanding these cycles helps us journey through love with a greater sense of confidence.

The foundation of Mindful Loving is grounded in our emotional health and our willingness to love and commit. Many factors impact the quality of our love relationships, including the relationships in our families of origin, past love relationships, and our level of emotional health and maturity. Mindful Loving embraces our physical, emotional, mental, sexual, and spiritual selves. The success of Mindful Loving is based on building trust, being vulnerable, and accepting ourselves and our partners.

Loving ourselves is vital to being able to love another. Mindful Loving is a mindset and practice that starts with the individual. It teaches us to stay open and reach greater levels of love and intimacy. Mindful Loving becomes second nature and enhances all our relationships. We all grow and change over time and the practice of Mindful Loving influences the very nature of our love relationships.

Mindful Loving is essential for creating a healthy and happy relationship. It is more than just a concept. It is a practice that translates into loving with passion and purpose.

In a Mindful Loving relationship every interaction reinforces the purpose of the relationship. When we feel loved, valued, understood, and desired, we are able to feel safe and nurtured. In Mindful Loving relationships, our passion is sustained.

Passion comes from the core of who we are. When we experience passion within ourselves, we are better able to create that passion in our love relationships. Everything we desire to experience around us must begin within us, and passion is no exception. When we experience passion within ourselves, we then create that passion in our Mindful Loving relationships.

Passion encompasses a wide range of strong emotions and includes both positive and negative emotions. Passion is the experience of joy; exhilaration; sexual fulfillment; ecstasy; and deep, abiding love. Passion fuels inspiration, fun and creativity and provides experiences that fulfill our desires. Passion invigorates our brains and gives life greater meaning. Having more passion in our Mindful Loving relationships means we create the relationships we desire, and experience love at deeper levels.

Passion is also the fuel for anger, disappointment, and frustration. The practice of Mindful Loving grounds us and helps us get through the tough and negative side of our passion. Our passion helps us determine our purpose as individuals and as partners.

Purpose comes from our reason for living and loving. Our purpose defines the way we live our lives and why we live those lives. Defining our purpose is a challenging and life-long task. It is one of the most meaningful inquiries we make during our lifetime. Some questions that clarify your purpose include the following:

- When do you feel most fulfilled, happy, or at peace?
- What would you like to do if you knew you would not fail?
- What do you stand for and what do you stand against?
- What would you like your legacy to be?
- What have you done or what do you want to do that would be most meaningful?

Understanding our purpose forms the basis of who we are, why we are driven to do what we do, and why and whom we love.

Knowing our own purpose is essential to developing the purpose for our Mindful Loving relationships. Understanding the purpose of our Mindful Loving relationships provides a solid foundation for our love relationships.

Some questions that help define the purpose of a Mindful Loving relationship are the following:

- What are our core values for our relationship?
- What is our vision for our relationship?
- Why are we together?
- As a couple, what do we stand for, and what do we stand against?
- Does our relationship give us a sense of peace and meaning?

Once we know the purpose of our Mindful Loving relationship, we have an opportunity to explore how to take it to heights and depths that are fulfilling and exhilarating. Knowing our purpose and the purpose of our Mindful Loving relationships deepens our love experience.

Through Mindful Loving relationships, we have the powerful experience of living with passion and purpose.

All of us desire connection, acceptance, and love. Mindful Loving is a way of loving that enables us to experience life and love more fully. We develop skills that help us love with greater passion and purpose. Mindful Loving calls us to be present and to prioritize the relationship by giving it time, attention, and care.

The two most common beliefs that affect our expectations in loving relationships are, "Couples should live happily ever after" and "Relationships are hard work." The first belief is based on a fairytale in which a prince and princess meet, fall in love, struggle, and then live happily ever after. Many people grow up believing this fairytale is true because the fantasy is reinforced by pop culture, books, and music. These people measure their relationships against the fantasy and feel disillusioned and disappointed when they fall short. These fairytales only reflect the beginning of the relationship, and we never see how the characters live together or manage their relationship after the story ends.

The other belief is "Relationships are hard work." This belief leads couples to live through struggles and challenges without developing skills for resolution and growth. These relationships are more practical in nature and less focused on passion and purpose. The truth is, although relationships do take work, they are more than "hard work". Mindful Loving relationships can also be fun and easy and provide us with greater passion and purpose.

We encourage you to rethink these two common beliefs. Think instead, that healthy, long-term relationships don't just happen. Relationships require attention, care, and meaningful work. This book is a guide that gives you the skills and tools to create your own Mindful Loving relationship.

When you do nothing to prioritize or strengthen your relationship, at best, it stays the same, or at worst, it begins to deteriorate. The goal of this book is to provide information based on our combined years of experience that will help you create a healthier, more fulfilling relationship with enhanced passion and purpose. It is not intended to be a substitute for psychotherapy or counseling. For those couples suffering from more complex problems, such as abuse, domestic violence, addiction, or mental health issues, this book can be a supplement to professional help.

Our current culture, with its technology, social media, global turmoil, and chronic stress can often distract us from being the kind of partners we want to be. We get caught up in fear and negativity and focus on what is wrong instead of what is right. At times, we neglect the practice of expressing and acknowledging appreciation and gratitude. Confronting problems or challenges in a relationship can feel overwhelming because we don't know where to start. This book is designed to help you make an honest assessment of where you are in your relationship, where you want to be, and gives you strategies and practical tools to get there. This guide will teach you to develop skills and practices that build healthy, passionate, and loving relationships.

There are three sections to *Mindful Loving: A Guide for Loving with Passion and Purpose:*

- **The Basics of Mindful Loving**. This section focuses on the two most important components of Mindful Loving, Loving Communication and Understanding & Respecting Differences.

- **Cycles of Mindful Loving**. This section helps couples' journey through the natural cycles of love relationships. Mindful Loving enables you to weather these cycles by acknowledging and accepting the ebb and flow of the cycles.

- **Practical Tools for Mindful Loving.** This section provides quick and simple activities and practices that enhance Mindful Loving relationships. These practical tools help you create your own relationship toolbox. This toolbox holds the skills and practical tools that help you grow and develop your own Mindful Loving relationship.

Partners engaged in Mindful Loving relationships include heterosexual and same-sex couples. The examples in this book reflect common patterns we have seen over the years. None of the examples are based on any one person or couple. We created the examples to illustrate concepts about relationship challenges and resolutions. We recognize they might appear simplistic or unrealistic. Couples resolve these challenges when they are committed, conscious and intentional in using the skills and practices of Mindful Loving.

We designed this book for couples and individuals. In addition to a focus on committed love relationships, it is also applicable for any relationship. Whether you are both committed to enriching your relationship or one of you is trying to change patterns in your relationship, this book will help you. We provide practical information as well as tools to assist you in your Mindful Loving journey.

There are several ways to use this book.

1. Read it and enjoy it.

   The goal of this book is to provide information that will help create a healthy and fulfilling relationship with enhanced passion and purpose.

2. Read and share the information with your partner.

   By sharing the information with your partner, you can discuss what resonates and apply it to your relationship.

3. Read the book with your partner.

   Reading the book together stimulates conversation. By discussing the information from each section, you will open yourselves up to new ideas, concepts, and practices.

4. Use it as a guide and workbook.

   Using this book as a guide and workbook means reading, discussing, and implementing new practices from each section. By implementing the skills and tools relevant to the growth of your relationship you can create your own Mindful Loving relationship and enhance your passion and purpose.

Mindful Loving is a practice that you develop over the life of your Mindful Loving relationship. It is a discipline that is worthwhile and becomes second nature and easier over time.

Mindful Loving: A Guide to Loving with Passion and Purpose teaches and empowers couples to sustain connection in their relationships. This connection allows passion to flourish and becomes the foundation for a relationship in which each partner feels loved, heard, understood, and desired. When passion flourishes, purpose is fulfilled, and Mindful Loving becomes one of life's greatest sources of joy and fulfillment.

CHAPTER 1

The Basics of Mindful Loving

The two basic components of Mindful Loving are Loving Communication and Understanding & Respecting Differences. Loving Communication is not something we are born with. It requires skills and tools that we learn and practice. Learning and using Loving Communication takes time and dedication.

Mindful Loving requires Understanding & Respecting Differences. People enter a Mindful Loving relationship as two separate and unique individuals. Mindful Loving recognizes our differences. When we talk about our differences, we learn to acknowledge and navigate the effects that differences have on our relationships.

Using the Basics of Mindful Loving, Loving Communication and Understanding & Respecting Differences provides the vehicle for connection and growth as individuals and as a couple. The relationship then becomes a safe haven where we honor and respect ourselves as well as our partners. Mindful Loving is a place where we live and express our passion for each other and life.

The purpose of Mindful Loving is for both partners to connect with their hearts, minds, and souls and embrace all that life has to offer. Mindful Loving can be enriching and restorative when partners master the skills for Loving Communication and Understanding & Respecting Differences as they move through the natural cycles of loving.

Loving Communication

Loving Communication is one of the basic components of Mindful Loving. Communication, verbal and non-verbal, is how we connect with one another. As humans, we all have an innate need to communicate. The practice of Loving Communication results in more trust, vulnerability, and acceptance. A Mindful Loving relationship provides a unique and intentional level of communication that is different from communication in any other relationship.

Loving Communication involves skills we can learn. It is important for us all to learn communication skills to enhance Mindful Loving. These communication skills enable clear, honest, and respectful communication, which results in greater love and intimacy. When communication is unclear, blaming, or defensive, it can lead to hurt, frustration, and fear, which can result in disillusionment and disconnection.

Through Loving Communication, we develop true intimacy with ourselves and our partners. One way of defining intimacy is "*into-me-see.*" This means we allow another to "see" us with greater honesty, depth, and detail. To allow another to truly "see" us, we first need to develop an intimate connection with ourselves. The most important relationship we have is with ourselves. We are, first and foremost, responsible for ourselves. The degree to which we love ourselves is the degree to which we can love another.

Love Yourself, and Be Responsible

Loving ourselves is a lifelong journey. The journey takes us through positive and negative experiences. Positive experiences are joyful, celebratory, and growth enhancing. These experiences increase our self-love and help define us. Negative experiences can be confusing and challenging. These experiences can tap into feelings of low self-esteem, shame, and negative thoughts and patterns.

Each of us has the responsibility to recognize our gifts and strengths as well as our challenges. Self-love grows when we accept those negative parts of ourselves, become mindful, and choose a different response that nurtures our self-love. We learn to value and respect ourselves by accepting and loving ourselves for who we really are.

When we love ourselves, we can then authentically value and respect our partners. When we are grounded in healthy self-love, it is impossible to do harm to another. Being grounded in self-love allows us to communicate openly and honorably with the intention of increasing respect and understanding.

Being responsible means, we are mindful of who we truly are and how we love ourselves and another person. When we stay conscious and responsible for our thoughts, feelings, and behaviors, love grows and has a collective impact on our family, our friends, and the world.

There are three skills that promote Loving Communication:

1. "I" Messages
2. Listen from the Heart to Understand
3. Communication Balance

Mindful Loving communication is about speaking respectfully, listening to understand, and ensuring a balance between speaking and listening.

1. "I" Messages

The first skill of Loving Communication is speaking "I" Messages. This skill enables us to speak respectfully. It is simply speaking about ourselves rather than about our partners. When we recognize and articulate our true thoughts and feelings, it is easier to use "I" Messages. "I" Messages help us tell our own stories and share our own feelings. It allows our partners to experience us more authentically.

"I" Messages help us take responsibility for our own experiences and own our own feelings. The intent of using "I" Messages is to communicate so our partners can understand what's going on with us.

Using "I" Messages helps create greater understanding and intimacy. When we take the time to really think about what and how we want to communicate, we are more apt to communicate without criticism and accusation.

An important way to practice "I" Messages is the expression of appreciation and gratitude.

The following are simple examples of appreciation and gratitude:

> "I appreciate your making dinner. I feel loved and cared about."
> "I love our snuggle time in the morning. It is a wonderful way to start the day."

Appreciation, whether we give it or receive it, lifts us up. Appreciation and gratitude are important aspects of a Mindful Loving relationship. They fuel our passion and connection to each other. The experience of feeling appreciation and gratitude is a rich and powerful nutrient for self-love and love for our partners. Purposefully choosing to think, feel, and express gratitude and appreciation amplifies our feelings of loving connection.

Consider the following question: In what ways do you show appreciation and gratitude?

We also can practice "I" Messages when we deal with conflict or negative interactions. It is easy to get caught up in the busyness of our lives and take each other for granted. When we get off balance it's easier for irritations and negative things to take a foothold in our minds and in our hearts. "I" Messages help us speak respectfully as we navigate through challenges and conflicts.

When we practice using "I" Messages, we become more aware of "You" Messages and the negative impact those messages can have on our communication. "I" Messages are messages we speak from our own authority, and "You" Messages are messages we speak presuming authority over our partners.

The following are examples of using "I" Messages and "You" Messages.

> Using an "I" Message, Vickie says, "I'm upset that you interrupted me when I was disciplining the children. It's really important to me that we support each other in our parenting."

Vickie is speaking about her feelings. We all have a right to feel upset. If we don't take a moment to examine what's going on for us, we might get sidetracked with accusations, criticisms, and false assumptions and use "You" Messages. When you start a statement with "You…" or "I think you are…," you are talking about your partner in a way that assumes you know about his or her experience. Using "You" Messages can lead to unloving and unhealthy communication because it results in a partner becoming defensive and responding with blame and excuses.

> Using a "You" Message, Vickie says, "You are such a pushover! I came home from work and found that Tina has her cell phone back! I can't believe you reneged on our consequence of taking away her cell phone. We agreed that she would lose her cell phone for a week."

> Ben responds with anger, "You are too strict. After all, she cleaned up the kitchen without being asked. She told me she needed to talk to some friends about homework. You never trust my ability to parent."

Criticism is one of the most destructive communication practices in a relationship. Criticism is a negative comment that passes judgment, censures, and focuses on fault finding. We know when we are heading down the rabbit hole of criticism when we begin interrupting each other with accusations and defending our positions.

Examples of criticism include the following:

- Name-calling: "You are a slob." "You are stupid." "You are a jerk, just like your father." Calling names is mean and hurtful, and can be abusive.

- Blaming: "You make me so mad (upset, crazy, angry, etc)." Blaming focuses on finding fault with the partner.

- Using BAT (Bad Absolutes as Truths) words such as:
  "You always…"
  "You never…"
  "Everybody…"
  "Nobody…"

  BATS words imply there is no other experience and intensifies or magnifies the situation.

- Asking questions that begin with *why* such as:
  "Why didn't you…?"
  "Why did you…?"
  "Why won't you…?"

  These imply blame and judgment and can only be responded to with a defense or an excuse.

Let's look at another example of "I" and "You" Messages. Consider the following scenario in which Debbie lashes out at Toby.

> Debbie and Toby have an ongoing battle about clothes being left on the floor. She feels angry, becomes critical, and says," You're such a slob. You know how important a clean house is to me. I think you are doing this on purpose just to make me mad."

Loving Communication skills enable Debbie to speak more respectfully. When she sees Toby's clothes on the floor, she becomes irritated. They have discussed this issue multiple times. She recognizes her own level of frustration and wants to lash out at him. Instead, she realizes she needs to take responsibility for her part. She resets herself by taking some deep breaths and realizes she has not effectively communicated the importance of having the clothes off the floor. She decides to use an "I" Message to communicate more effectively.

Using an "I" Message, she says," I feel frustrated when I find your dirty clothes on the floor because we have talked about this before. I would appreciate it if you would put your clothes in the hamper."

This enables Toby to accept responsibility, and he responds, "You're right. I'm sorry. I'll pick them up right now. I didn't realize it made you feel that way. I will work harder to pick up my messes."

"I" Messages are a necessary skill used to manage conflict in healthy ways. The intention of Loving Communication is to generate understanding, acceptance, and resolution. Disagreements and conflicts are normal parts of all loving relationships. We all experience differences with our partners; some will lead to conflict, and others will not.

When we are confronted with disagreements and conflict, it is important to first take responsibility for our own part in the conflict. As demonstrated by Debbie before she spoke to Toby, we need to acknowledge our feelings and our part in the conflict, reset, and choose the most effective communication.

When you face difficult or emotionally charged situations, some good questions to ask yourself to respond more effectively are the following:

1. What is my part in this conflict?
2. Is there something I need to first resolve and release within myself?
3. What do I think my partner's part is in this conflict?
4. What do I want to happen to resolve this conflict?
5. How do I release the emotional charge?
6. Am I willing to forgive and let it go?

We also can use "I" Messages when making a request or asking a question. "I" Messages enable us to take responsibility and be more honest with our requests and questions. To be more responsible and honest, use the following guideline:

When asking a question, first answer the question for yourself to clarify the information you are seeking.

This means that when asking a question, we need to stop, think, and answer that question for ourselves first. Usually, we ask questions to gather information. Many questions are not purely information seeking; if the person asking the question might have another agenda. People often ask questions to receive validation, hide criticism, or express indirect desires.

The skill of answering your own question first allows you to be clear about the real intention of the question.

Consider the following example:

Peyton wants to ask Mo," Do you want to go out to dinner?"

Before she asks the question, Peyton needs to check in with herself. She determines that she doesn't just want to go to dinner; she wants to go out for Mexican food. This assessment allows her to take responsibility and be more honest with Mo. She then can say, "Mo, I am hungry and would like to go out for Mexican food. Are you up for going out with me?"

Mo then understands that the question is about going out for Mexican food, not just going out to dinner.

Consider another example:

Chrystal asks Zach, "Do you like my new dress?"

This question leaves Zach vulnerable and uncomfortable, and he does not know what to say. He wonders, "does she want the truth?"" Is she looking for a compliment?" "What is she really wanting?"

However, if Chrystal first asks herself, "Do I like my dress?" she might realize she is not sure about the color. She is then clearer about asking his opinion and says, "Zach, I would like your opinion. I am not sure about the color of my dress. It might be too bold for me. What do you think?"

This gives Zach more information, and he replies, "I do like the dress. I agree with you, that it might be better in a softer color."

Chrystal took responsibility for her uncertainty and was clear about wanting Zach's honest opinion. Zach felt more comfortable in responding because Chrystal was clear about what she was asking.

Another common example is the following:

Kevin comes home and sees that Chris has not fulfilled his promise to clean the kitchen. Kevin asks Chris, "Did you clean the kitchen?"

It is obvious the kitchen has not been cleaned, and Chris feels irritated and criticized.

He feels snarky and responds, "What do you think?"

This leads to further tension, and Kevin yells, "You said you were going to clean the kitchen! I can never count on you to do what you say you are going to do!"

Kevin catches himself being critical and stops to ask himself what he wants. He determines that he feels disappointed and irritated that Chris didn't follow through with what he said he was going to do. He takes responsibility for his angry outburst and says, "I am sorry I yelled at you. When I came home and saw that the kitchen was a mess, I felt angry. I trusted you when you said it would be taken care of before I got home. Let's do a do over. Would you please clean up the kitchen before we start dinner?"

Chris acknowledges Kevin's frustration and apologizes for not keeping his word, He says," I understand you feel let down. I can clean the kitchen now."

When Kevin stopped himself and expressed his feelings without criticism, Chris was able to respond in a more understanding and loving way. They stayed connected through what used to be a repetitive fight.

Some other common questions used to criticize, and express indirect desires include the following:

- "Did you eat all the left-overs?" might really mean "You ate the leftovers and didn't leave any for me."
- "Is that a new outfit?" might mean "I'm upset that you are not following our budget this month."
- "What time is it?" might mean "We are running late and need to hurry."
- "Did you take the garbage out?" might really mean "Do I always have to be the one to remind you to take the garbage out?"
- "Are you cold?" might really mean "I'm cold. Will you turn up the heat?"

Consider the following questions: Do you recognize any of these questions? What are your questions, and how can you answer your questions first?

2. Listen from the Heart to Understand

The second skill of Loving Communication is Listen from the Heart to Understand. Listening to understand what our partners are saying is a skill we develop when we listen from our heart.

The key to Listen from the Heart to Understand means putting your reactions and responses aside to really hear what your partner has to say. It's a little bit like putting yourself in your partner's shoes, trying to understand exactly what's going on. It allows you to confirm what your partner is saying and reach a greater level of understanding about your partner's experience and story.

This helps you to fully imagine and understand what your partner's experience is without judging or editing. You learn to suspend your own story and reaction in that moment and truly engage and connect with your partner.

It is also important to really listen and believe what your partner says instead of believing in what you think you know about your partner. Believing that you know what is going on with your partner without really listening to what he or she is saying about the experience can be disrespectful and dangerous. When your experience or feeling is different from your partner's, it is critical that you believe and accept what your partner is saying about himself or herself. This practice of believing what your partner is saying helps decrease assumptions and increase acceptance. The skill of Listening from the Heart to Understand builds trust in the relationship.

Believe what your partner shares about his or her experience.

In life, everyone gets to be the world's best authority on one thing: himself or herself. It is important that in the relationship, both partners recognize and accept that each is the expert on himself or herself.

When you believe your partner is telling the truth about his or her experience and feelings, the most loving thing you can do is listen.

An example of believing your partner is the following:

> When Justin turned forty, he told Susan he was struggling with getting older and did not want to do anything special to celebrate his birthday. Susan loves parties and planned a huge surprise party. On the day of the party, Justin was gracious. After it was over, he told Susan how upset he was that she had disregarded his wishes.
>
> Susan initially felt hurt, but then she recognized how difficult it was for Justin to be honest with her about his party. When she listened from her heart, she realized Justin had spoken his truth about not wanting a party and she had not believed him. She had

operated on her own assumptions, neglecting to respect his wishes. When she apologized, Justin received the best gift of all: being believed and respected.

Susan let go of her assumption that her enjoyment of parties would also be fun for Justin. When she let go of her assumption, she was able to accept and believe that Justin did not want a party.

We have all heard the adage when we assume, "when we make an ass out of u and me." Over time, it is easy to slip into assuming that we know everything there is to know about our partners and ourselves.

Assumptions are detours from authenticity.

It is understandable that we generalize and make deductions from information, but it is important to check that information out. We often rely on efficiency, not accuracy, for our thoughts. Our thoughts become unchecked beliefs that lead to assumptions. Once we learn to let go of assumptions, we make room to explore all the possibilities of what is really going on.

Exploring takes time and energy and results in clearer communication and deeper understanding. As we let go of assumptions, we become more accepting of our partners' truth and real voices. Acceptance is the pause button and reset button for maintaining Loving Communication.

One of the toughest challenges of this skill, Listen from the Heart to Understand, is to use it when your partner is saying something negative about you. The key to listening from the heart is to listen, not to speak. The goal is to listen to really understand what is being said and how your partner is feeling. The experience of being heard and understood is profound and creates a depth of emotional connection, safety, and security.

This skill is challenging. When you hear a negative comment, a natural response is to defend or explain yourself. It takes time, attention, and care to stop the habit of a defensive response and use the skill of Listen from the Heart to Understand.

In the earlier example, Debbie told Toby about her frustration with his leaving his clothes on the floor.

> Toby wants to respond with explanations and excuses, he stops, takes a deep breath, and practices the skill, Listen from the Heart to Understand. He follows these steps:
>
> 1. Hear and express your partner's feeling. This is the first and most important part of using the skill.
>
> 2. Recognize and accept responsibility for the behavior.
>
> 3. Check-in to provide acknowledgment, clarification, and acceptance.
>
> Toby says, "I understand you are frustrated [step 1] because I left my dirty clothes on the floor, even though we have already talked about it [step 2]. Is that right [step 3]?"
>
> Debbie nods and responds, "Yes, that is exactly what I mean. I really want to talk about this and come up with a solution that will stop us from recycling this fight. Thank you for listening." Debbie feels validated and heard.
>
> Toby did not try to defend or explain why he left the clothes on the floor. His response was to listen and confirm what he heard Debbie say.

When we respond with an understanding of our partners' experience first, our response allows our partners to feel heard and validated. Toby's response does not mean he agrees with Debbie; it tells her that he hears her. This skill helps us build greater understanding, intimacy, and trust. It is not easy to stop defending or explaining our behavior and just listen to what is being said, using these skills creates a bridge between conflict and resolution.

Consider the following question: When was the last time you really listened from your heart to understand and learned something new about your partner?

3. Communication Balance

The third skill of Loving Communication is achieving Communication Balance, the balance between speaking and listening. It is important to understand and respect both the speaker and the listener.

It is common for both partners to talk and try to listen at the same time. Often, while listening to our partners, we are constructing our own response to what is being said. Doing this means it is impossible to fully listen and understand what our partners are saying and understand his or her experiences.

An example of Communication Balance is the following:

> Elizabeth talks to Blake about his use of his cell phone at dinner and says, "I wish you wouldn't use your cell phone at the dinner table. I think it is a bad example for the kids."

> Before she has a chance to finish, Blake interrupts and says, "I don't know what you're complaining about. You are always on your phone checking Facebook. What kind of example is that?"

> Blake notices Elizabeth's irritated expression and realizes his mistake. He says, "Let's both take a deep breath and start over. You want to talk about my use of the cell phone during dinner, right? I am willing to listen."

> Elizabeth appreciates Blake's Loving Communication and says, "Okay, let me try this again. Both of us could do better about managing technology. I would like us to make a family policy of no cell phones at the dinner table because dinner is a time for

us to connect with one another as a family. What do you think about that?"

Blake responds, "I like that idea. I can do that."

Communication Balance is a skill that requires patience. It involves a disciplined monologue wherein one person speaks, and the other person listens. Loving Communication always requires a balance between speaking and listening. Communication Balance ensures that each partner speaks without interruption. When there is Communication Balance, the message becomes clearer, and the listener can hear and understand what is being said. With this balance, partners then switch roles: the speaker becomes the listener, and the listener becomes the speaker.

Another example of Communication Balance:

Caroline was upset about Lance getting home late from work. He told her he expected to be home at seven o'clock. She prepared a special dinner and was looking forward to spending a nice evening together. She was hurt and angry when he called at seven forty-five to say he would be home late. Feeling angry, she left the dinner for him to warm up and decided to go to bed.

She knew that the intensity of her feelings needed time to settle. The next morning, she asked if they could talk.

Caroline told Lance she was hurt and angry because she believed he'd chosen to be at work instead of being with her. She told him she had been looking forward to spending time together, and the evening had been ruined. She was furious he hadn't bothered to call until nearly an hour after he'd said he would be home.

Lance listened to Caroline without interruption and focused his attention on fully understanding her perspective and feelings. He kept a check on his desire to defend himself and explain that he had been on an important, unexpected phone call that prevented him from contacting her. As he listened from his heart to understand, he began to understand what waiting for him had been like for Caroline. He listened to her disappointment about their not spending time together. He looked into her eyes, moved closer to her, and responded, "So, when I am late and don't call you, you begin to believe that my work is more important than you?"

That statement helped Caroline feel heard. Her anger and hurt melted and tears filled her eyes. In that moment, she felt close and connected to Lance. Lance felt good about listening to Caroline and felt relieved and more connected to her.

After feeling heard, Caroline asked Lance to tell her about what had happened at work that made him late. She was ready to listen to him and his experience of being late. Lance took the opportunity to tell Caroline about his frustration over being stuck at work and having to let her down.

They continued their conversation and discussed strategies to prevent this situation from happening again. They agreed that Lance would call or text if he was going to be late.

Communication Balance is especially important when there is conflict or hurt feelings are present. When there is Communication Balance, wherein one person speaks while the other person listens, couples experience reconnection through managing their conflict effectively, reaffirming their commitment, and sustaining their love connection.

Loving Communication involves these three skills: "I" Messages, Listen from the Heart to Understand, and Communication Balance. These skills provide opportunities to be present, thoughtful, and accepting. They are core qualities of Mindful Loving and result in being loving and feeling loved. The use of these Loving Communication skills builds a solid foundation. This foundation supports our passion and purpose. Our Mindful Loving relationships gets stronger and stronger as we continue to build trust, share vulnerabilities, and accept ourselves and each other.

Consider the following exercise: When was a time when you felt heard and accepted by your partner and share the story with your partner.

Understanding & Respecting Differences

The practice of Understanding & Respecting Differences is the second basic component of Mindful Loving. People enter a Mindful Loving relationship as two separate and unique individuals. It is important to recognize how our differences enhance as well as diminish our comfort and connection with each other. Understanding & Respecting Differences enables us to navigate through the many changes, challenges, and celebrations of life.

When we practice this skill, passion and purpose come alive. When we practice Understanding & Respecting Differences, we engage with the real challenge and depth of our purpose to connect and love each other. Meeting this challenge unleashes a passion that enables us to experience life and love more fully.

Understanding & Respecting Differences in Mindful Loving involves three important skills:

1. Follow the Golden Rule of Mindful Loving.
2. Be Each Other's Go-To Person.
3. Manage Differences with Love and Respect.

1. Follow the Golden Rule of Mindful Loving

The first skill for Understanding & Respecting Differences is the Golden Rule of Mindful Loving. The Golden Rule, "Do unto others as you would have them do unto you," means we treat and love others the way we want to be treated and loved. The Golden Rule is a universal principle that helps us live our lives with tolerance, consideration, and compassion.

Mindful Loving requires an expansion of the traditional Golden Rule. The Golden Rule of Mindful Loving is this: "Love your partner the way your partner wants to be loved." This means you treat and love your partner the way he or she wants to be treated instead of how you want to be treated and loved.

We first need to identify how we want to be loved, and then we can teach our partners how to love us. Without using the Golden Rule of Mindful Loving, we typically operate from the traditional Golden Rule. With good intentions, we treat our partners the way we want to be treated, not necessarily the way they want to be treated. This difference can cause problems.

An example of using the Golden Rule of Mindful Loving is the following:

> Both Molly and Will care about each other, but they missed the mark when it came to taking care of each other when they were sick. When Molly got the flu, Will's way of loving and caring for her was to leave her alone and wait for her to ask for his help. This made Molly feel even worse, as she thought Will was ignoring her and not giving her the care she wanted.
>
> When Will got the flu, Molly showered him with constant care and attention. This made Will feel frustrated because all he wanted was to be left alone.
>
> After recovering, Will suggested that they talk about how to care for each other when they are ill. Using their Loving Communication skills, they learned that they were missing the mark in taking care of each other.
>
> Molly recognized how much she loves to get attention when she is sick. Will, on the other hand, recognized he wants to be left alone when he gets sick. During this conversation, they came to understand and respect their differences and each other's needs.

Using the Golden Rule of Mindful Loving Will agreed to give Molly the kind of care and attention she needed, and Molly agreed to be patient and wait for Will to request her help when he was sick.

In another example, Mary and John learned to take responsibility for what was most important to them and implemented the Golden Rule of Mindful Loving.

> After three years of marriage, John and Mary settled into the rhythm of married life, learning about each other in ways that were sometimes challenging and unpredictable. One of the things that John loved most about Mary was her ability to attend and respond to his needs. One of the things Mary loved most about John was the way he helped her feel safe, secure, and respected.
>
> When Mary wanted to decorate their new home, John became resistant and irritated. He realized Mary's desire to spend money on decorating triggered his fear about financial security. He was already worried about their large mortgage payment and felt as if they had just signed their life away. When he criticized Mary for wanting to spend more money on decorating, she felt confused, hurt, and disrespected. She dealt with her feelings by withdrawing emotionally and sexually.
>
> John was confused by her withdrawal and protected himself by also becoming more distant. Thus, the dance of disconnection began.
>
> Their growing distance became increasingly uncomfortable for Mary. She texted John and asked for some time to talk after work. John felt relieved at Mary's request and was ready to find a way to reconnect. Their commitment to Mindful Loving enabled them both to recognize their own part in the disharmony and seek resolution and reconnection.
>
> At their meeting, Mary recognized that her withdrawal hurt John, and she wanted to reach out and reconnect with him. John talked about his fear of not having enough money and his desire to be a good provider for Mary. He apologized for his critical comments. He then told her that he really did share her excitement about their new home but feared the cost of the decorating would put them in

debt. Instead of criticizing Mary, he expressed a more honest and vulnerable part of himself by sharing his fear.

Mary listened from her heart to understand without interrupting John. She was able to understand and respect John's feelings. She apologized for shutting down and withdrawing from him.

Through their loving conversation and use of the Golden Rule of Mindful Loving, John appreciated Mary's ability to understand him, which rekindled his feelings of being loved. Mary restored her trust in his acceptance of what she wanted, which rekindled her sense of safety and security. They created a list of items that Mary wanted for the home, and together they prioritized the purchasing of the items. Thus, the dance of reconnection began.

To teach your partner how you want to be loved, you first need to know what you want. Many people have not defined this for themselves and expect their partners to just magically know what they want. Many share a common and unrealistic belief that states: "If you really loved me, you would know what I need and want." It is important to take the time to find out what you want and not expect your partner to be a mind reader.

Once you determine what you want, communicate that information clearly to your partner. Then ask your partner how he or she wants to be treated and loved. Even if you have a good idea about how your partner wants to be loved, it is necessary to check it out.

When implementing the Golden Rule of Mindful Loving, keep the following in mind:

1. Recognize what you want and first ask yourself, "How do I want to be loved or treated?"
2. Take responsibility and use Loving Communication skills to communicate how you want to be treated.
3. Ask your partner how he or she wants to be loved and treated.

Using the Golden Rule of Mindful Loving gives us valuable information. With practice, you learn how to give and receive love in the most meaningful and respectful ways.

2. Be Each Other's Go-To Person

The second important skill in Understanding & Respecting Differences is Be Each Other's Go-To Person. Your Go-To Person is someone you trust to love you and be there for you. It is the one person, above all others, with whom you share your most intimate experiences. In Mindful Loving, partners advocate for each other. They stand by and support each other in the face of adversity.

Partners need to practice being each other's Go-To Person when dealing with each other's families and friends. One of the ways to Be Each Other's Go-To Person involves moving your relationship allegiance from the family of origin to the love relationship with your partner. In these relationships with family and friends, partners are often challenged to be the champion for one another.

Our early life experiences with family and friends are important pieces of the fabric of our lives. It is helpful for each of us to be curious and understand how those relationships have shaped us.

Consider the following example of Be Each Other's Go-To Person:

> Caleb and his wife, Cindy, were excited to visit Caleb's hometown over the Christmas holiday. Since his last visit home, he's gotten married, and has two children, and established a successful career. He was grateful to his parents for inviting his new family to share holiday stories and traditions from his childhood.
>
> He acted as Cindy's Go-To Person when she expressed a sadness about not having their own tradition of reading special holiday books to their children on Christmas Eve. He advocated for her and talked to his parents about adding that tradition to their

Christmas Eve activities. His parents were delighted to add the new tradition of reading the holiday stories to their grandchildren.

Getting together with his friends was a different experience. Caleb connected with some of his friends who lived a similar lifestyle and had growing families and careers. Sadly, some of his other friends seemed stuck in the past, still focused on drinking and partying. Cindy acted as Caleb's Go-To Person when Caleb expressed his disappointment and sadness about those friends. His excitement about sharing meaningful time with those friends was dampened. Cindy helped him sort through his feelings, and he realized that nothing but memories connected him with those friends now. Cindy supported him as he struggled with letting go of some of his past.

By being each other's Go-To Person, partners respect and accept the influence of each other's family and friends. When we accept that this influence exists, we are then less likely to experience in-law horror stories and loyalty conflicts with old friends. It is important to back each other up and be each other's Go-To Person in managing these influences.

When partners are each other's Go-To Person, they have intimate and private information about each other. It is important to respect this privileged information and ask permission before sharing personal information with others.

It is a frequent practice for people to talk with friends and family about their relationships. Both men and women often share specific and intimate information about their relationships. Although the intention might be innocent, sharing this information without permission might inadvertently do harm to a Mindful Loving relationship.

Consider the following examples of failure to respect personal and privileged information:

Ainsley talked to Jane about the fight she'd had with her partner, Monique. Ainsley told Jane that Monique spent too much money gambling at the casino. Ainsley was upset and complained that she and Monique were on a tight budget, and she didn't think Monique was very responsible when it came to spending money. Monique was hurt when she found out Ainsley had shared this personal information with Jane.

In another example:

Becky talks to her friend, Mary, about difficulties she's having in her sexual relationship with her husband, Marco. She complains that Marco usually comes too quickly and does not give her enough time to reach her own orgasm. When Becky and Marco have dinner with Mary and her husband, Becky realizes that Marco will feel hurt if he knows she shared that intimate detail of their relationship.

Another example:

Ron uses stories about his wife's failures and mishaps in the kitchen to bring attention and humor to the office. These stories soon became a regular topic of conversation. He never realizes that sharing these stories could deeply offend and hurt his wife.

Don't assume that it's okay to share personal information without your partner's permission. Sharing information can be a violation of the integrity and trust in the relationship.

It is important to talk to your partner first and discuss guidelines for sharing privileged information with others. Be sensitive, and let your partner know when you have shared details of your relationship with others.

Have an honest discussion about sharing information in the following areas: finances, your sexual relationship, fights and frustrations and secrets you have shared with each other. Discuss what topics are off limits to share with others.

The skill of being each other's Go-To Person enables you to prioritize each other. As you become more respectful of what information is shared outside the relationship, you experience greater intimacy and trust in Mindful Loving.

3. Manage Differences with Love and Respect

The third skill for Understanding & Respecting Differences is Manage Differences with Love and Respect. As two individuals, partners come together to create a loving union. They experience similarities as well as differences. The differences can serve to enrich and complement each other. Some of the differences couples experience are in religion and spirituality, culture and lifestyle, personality and age, and brain and sexuality.

Differences in religion and spiritual practices can be one of the most challenging differences to manage. Consider the following example:

> Brennan grew up Catholic, and Rebecca grew up Jewish. Up until they had children, they were able to easily manage their religious differences. When they had their first son, they were confronted with the significance of their different religious backgrounds and its impact on their new family.

> Their first challenge was in deciding about circumcision. Rebecca's family strongly encouraged her to have a traditional bris ceremony. Brennan wanted his son to be circumcised in the hospital. They were both surprised by their strong desire to follow traditions from their own families. They had never expected their different religious backgrounds to be a problem in making decisions about their children.

> This was the beginning of exploring the depth of their different religious backgrounds and what they wanted for their children. They both agreed they wanted to provide their children with rich and meaningful religious experiences.

As Brennan and Rebecca discovered, sometimes differences that are not significant early in the relationship can become difficult challenges later. Through Loving Communication, they were able to negotiate and reach a compromise. They invited the rabbi to come to the hospital to perform the circumcision.

Differences in culture and lifestyle need to be managed with love and respect, as well as with understanding. Here is an example:

Don and Jacque met at a work-related conference in Los Angeles. Don was first-generation Korean and grew up in Los Angeles, with all the diversity and opportunities of a big city. Jacque grew up in a small rural town in Idaho in a community that provided her with a deep sense of security. Her family was rooted in the rich culture of many generations of farmers.

After they married, Jacque wanted to move back to her hometown to raise their family. She and Don discussed the benefits and challenges of making such a significant lifestyle change which led them to the decision to move.

After settling into the new lifestyle, Don was surprised to find he adapted quickly because of the warmth and acceptance of this new community. Jacque understood the importance of Don's Korean heritage. She committed to learning more about his traditions and integrated those into their life together. Through Loving Communication, they honored their differences and created a deeper understanding and respect for each other.

Don and Jacque learned that their differences served to expand and broaden their life together. Don, who had only known living in a big city, was able to experience a different way of living. Jacque loved integrating Korean customs into their life together. Accepting and respecting differences along with understanding each other opened them to a new and enriching life.

Managing differences in personality and age requires flexibility and patience. Consider the following example:

> Judy and Mike have been married for more than thirty years. Judy, now fifty-five, describes herself as a free spirit. Mike is sixty-eight and describes himself as a loveable control freak. Judy thrives on spontaneity and admits she has never enjoyed organizing and cleaning the house. Mike, on the other hand, thrives on order and organization. Over the years, they have been creative in managing their differences. For example, Judy and Mike planned a so-called yes day every quarter. On their yes day, they say yes to any spontaneous, unplanned adventures that either suggests. Similarly, they scheduled quarterly cleanup days when they both participate in organizing and purging clutter in the home.
>
> When Mike retired and found himself spending more time at home, the loveable control freak transformed into a critical complainer. He found the chronic clutter and piles of mail on the kitchen counter to be a constant irritant and began to lose his patience. When Judy came home from work, she was met with criticism and complaints about her housekeeping. The stress in the relationship continued until Mike reached a breaking point and told Judy they needed to talk.
>
> Even though the conversation had a rough start, they stopped and remembered to use the Loving Communication skills that had helped them throughout their marriage. They both recognized that the changes created by his retirement had intensified old challenges that now needed to be addressed.
>
> They resolved some of these challenges when Judy recognized the difficulty Mike was having in spending so much more time at home. Mike became more patient when he realized that Judy was still dealing with the stress of working every day. Together they produced creative solutions that helped them manage their differences not only with love and respect but also with greater flexibility and patience.

Managing differences in brain and sexual functioning requires us to expand our knowledge and appreciate the complexity of our brains and bodies.

Through ongoing advances in neuroscience and psychology, we are learning about how the structure and wiring variations in the male and female brains create differences in how men and women process the world. There are some structural and hormonal differences, but most importantly, the way our brains process information contributes to the confusion and difficulty in loving relationships.

The male brain processes information internally; a man thinks to himself, and typically deals with decision-making in a practical and logical manner by activating his left brain first. The left brain in the male is the seat of logic, language, and linear thinking. He utilizes his right brain for processing emotions, creativity, and verbal communication. Consider the following example:

> Adam and Alice have decided to replace their bathroom faucet. Each of them engages in his or her unique decision-making process.
>
> Adam first accesses from his left brain. He removes the old faucet to determine what is needed to replace the faucet. He then goes on the internet to research viable options. Overwhelmed by the plethora of choices for new faucets, he thinks, *The old faucet worked fine, I just need to find one like the old one.* Before he makes the final decision, his right brain kicks in as he considers how Alice will feel about the choice. He concludes, *A faucet is a faucet, and it needs no emotional attachment.* He tells Alice about the faucet he plans to get and is comfortable with his decision.

The female brain processes information by talking out loud and typically deals with decision-making in a logical and emotional manner by simultaneously activating both the right and left hemispheres of the brain. The female also uses many more words per day than the male. On an average day, a female might speak up to twenty thousand words, while a male who might speak up to only seven thousand words.

> When Alice hears his decision, she wants to talk about it before he purchases the new faucet. She starts by saying, "Okay, but I need to know more details about the new faucet. Over the years, we have made a lot of changes to update the bathroom, and I would like to go to the store and to see all the new styles and look at a new mirror and towel racks as well. I was at Cheryl's the other day and really liked their new faucets. Do you want to swing by her place first?"

> When Adam hears about all the details, he feels overwhelmed because he had zeroed in on a singular aspect of the project, just replacing the old faucet. Alice does not understand how he could have ignored all these important parts of the decision. They realized they needed to use their Loving Communication skills to come to a mutual decision about the new faucet.

By Understanding & Respecting Differences, Adam and Alice realized that they each had a unique way of approaching the same decision. When Alice talked about the extraneous details of the project, Adam learned to be patient. Alice learned to respect Adam's ability to focus and complete one task at a time. They listened to each other's perspective and produced a plan that met both of their needs.

Understanding our brain differences enables us to communicate our wants and needs more clearly. It is important to remember that men and women process information differently as we work together to make decisions. Consider the following example:

> Tessa and Jonah are having a conversation about eating.

> Tessa says, "I'm hungry."

> Jonah says, "I am hungry too. Where do you want to go eat?"

Tessa, using both hemispheres of her brain, begins talking out loud, asking questions about what they want to eat and where they want to go. She says, "I like Mexican food. Let's go to our favorite Mexican food restaurant."

Jonah, checking with his left brain, realizes that Mexican food would satisfy his hunger, and he says, "Okay, let's eat Mexican food."

Then, Tessa says, "No, I'm going to eat Mexican food tomorrow for lunch. Why don't we go to the Italian restaurant?"

Jonah sends information to his brain, assesses, *I like Italian food*, changes gears, and says, "Okay, let's eat Italian."

Tessa is not finished making her decision and is still processing out loud. She says, "Oh wait. I have a coupon for a new restaurant that just opened down the street. Let's try it out."

By this time, Jonah is exasperated and says, "Just make up your mind, and let's go eat!"

Does this sound familiar to you? This common example illustrates how Jonah and Tessa approached this decision differently. As Tessa is a female, her decision-making process includes her feelings and multiple details that are important to her. Jonah's decision-making process is simply focused on just getting something to eat.

It is important for both Tessa and Jonah to understand that they approach decision-making in different ways. Jonah is learning to wait until Tessa is finished processing her decision. If he jumps on her first response, eating Mexican food, he might end up confused and very frustrated. When he understands that her decision-making process is different from his, he can wait until she has reached her final answer and not attach to her other options.

Tessa, on the other hand, understands that when Jonah opens his mouth, he has reached his final answer. She is learning to respect his frustration with her decision-making process. She helps him by reminding him to be patient with her as she is, thinking out loud, and clarifies for him when she has reached her final answer.

Managing differences in our sexual functioning provides opportunities to enhance the intimacy and connection in our Mindful Loving relationships. There is a common belief that when people love each other, they will each sustain the same level of sexual passion and desire throughout the relationship. We all experience differences in our sensual and sexual expression over the course of our time together. Men and women experience significant sensual and sexual differences that are a result of hormonal and brain differences. Some of these sex differences in same-sex relationships are present but might not be directly related to brain and hormonal differences.

It is common to experience differences in our sexual functioning. Some of these differences include:

- sensual desire and sexual passion,
- energy and timing for sexual activity, and
- reasons and purpose for having sex.

The most common and difficult sexual differences are differences in libido and desire. There are times or moments in our love relationships when we are in sync with our sexual desires and passion. There are also times or moments when we are out of sync. When couples experience desire and libido differences, it can be a painful experience for both partners. Talking about our sensual desires and our sexual passion helps us stay open and honest with ourselves and each other.

Consider the following scenario:

> Timothy jokes about his high libido and how he could have sex anytime and anywhere. Sasha is more sexually inhibited. She grew up in a conservative family in which sex was taboo and never

discussed. She loves Timothy and feels safe in the relationship. She is willing to explore and share her own sensual and sexual desires with him. Timothy is learning to manage his sexual energy so together they can create their own unique dance of sexual passion and pleasure.

Managing differences in energy and timing for sexual activity requires honest communication and negotiation. Many couples find they have little energy left over for lovemaking after a busy day. Fatigue is the most common cause of a decrease in energy for sexual activity.

Synchronizing time and prioritizing sexual activity become challenging as couples deal with work, children, social activities, and household chores. Consider the following example:

> Mitch gets up at four o'clock every day to go to his landscaping job. Starting early allows him to pick up his three children after school. He spends time helping them with homework and coaching their soccer team. His wife, Addison, gets the children off to school and then goes to her high-stress job as a medical office manager.
>
> It is often eight o'clock in the evening before Mitch and Addison have time to even see each other and catch up at the end of the day. Their schedules and activities leave them both exhausted, and they have little energy for sexual connection. The best solution for them is to schedule sex on Saturday or Sunday mornings before the kids get up.

It is normal and acceptable to have sex for different reasons. Some of the varied reasons are as follows:

- To demonstrate our love for each other
- To connect
- To relieve sexual tension, stress, and boredom
- To have a child
- To keep the relationship healthy
- To combat the fear of losing the relationship

- To make up from a fight
- To have fun

Just as appetites for foods might change over time, appetites for sexual experiences might change as well. Some things to talk about include the following:

1. What is your expectation about the frequency and quality of sexual connection?
2. How do you each experience sexual pleasure?
3. How do you keep your sexual activity hot and spicy?
4. Are you both satisfied with the current state of your sexual experience?

Some reasons for having sex are influenced by how we are feeling about ourselves, our partner, and our relationship. When we recognize that we are experiencing differences in reasons for having sex, or not having sex, these questions can be helpful to talk about:

1. How are you feeling about my body image and expressing your sexual self?
2. Are you prioritizing your time and energy for sex?
3. Are you feeling happy, angry, or resentful?
4. Do you feel emotionally connected to your partner, or is there emotional disconnection?

Consider the following example of sexual disconnection:

> Penny is experiencing menopausal symptoms, such as hot flashes, insomnia, and irritability. She has gained thirty pounds and is disgusted with her body image. She is feeling disconnected from Max and realizes she has been carrying a load of resentment toward him for not talking with her and for not being more helpful around the house.
>
> Max feels defeated and resentful and spends his free time in his man cave, drinking beer and watching sports.

Their built-up resentment for each other has created a wall that blocks their ability to connect emotionally and sexually. After attending a marriage-enrichment seminar at their church, they both realized they need some help to reignite their emotional and sexual connections. Their pastor helps them start talking to each other. They are able to speak and release their hurts and resentment. Their emotional reconnection leads to a rekindling of their sex life.

Understanding & Respecting Differences in our brain and sexual functioning enables us to enhance our emotional and sexual intimacy. Clear and nonjudgmental communication is key to managing our differences with love and respect.

Understanding & Respecting Differences is an important skill in Mindful Loving. Open, honest, and loving conversations about our differences are necessary to bridge our differences and maintain loving connections. Trust, vulnerability, and acceptance are the ingredients for continuing to build passion and purpose in our Mindful Loving relationships.

CHAPTER 2

Cycles of Mindful Loving

There are natural cycles in all Mindful Loving relationships. The skillful practice and use of the basic components of Mindful Loving, Loving Communication, and Understanding & Respecting Differences, enables us to move through these natural cycles with more confidence and ease. We move through natural cycles of harmony, stability, and predictability, as well as cycles of disharmony, instability, and unpredictability. When we understand these cycles of loving, we learn to develop and maintain healthy emotional connections.

The following are the primary Cycles of Mindful Loving:

- The First Cycle of Mindful Loving is characterized by love and attraction. It is like springtime. We experience new beginnings and renewal.

- The Second Cycle of Mindful Loving is characterized by love and acceptance. It is like summer. Our love deepens, and we experience greater discovery, acceptance, and intimacy.

- The Third Cycle of Mindful Loving is characterized by love and transition. It is like the fall. We experience moments of loss or sadness as we move through personal, professional, and life-stage transitions.

- The Fourth Cycle of Mindful Loving is characterized by love and resilience. It is like winter. We turn inward, and take time for reflection, and experience a deepening of our love connection.

Nature cycles through the four seasons every year, providing us with experiences that we know and expect. We know that every year, summer is followed by fall, and winter is followed by spring. The Cycles of Mindful

Loving are just as natural, predictable, and unique as the cycles in nature. As in nature, these Cycles of Mindful Loving are repeated and revisited over the course of the lifetime of the relationship. Unlike in nature, the timing and duration of the Cycles of Mindful Loving vary. Some couples stay in the first cycle of love and attraction for years. Other couples initially move through the first cycle more quickly as they adjust to having children or blending families. These couples stay in the second cycle of love and acceptance for longer periods of time as their children grow and develop. The timing of the third cycle of love and transition might occur naturally or unexpectedly as couples face changes, such as health changes, career transitions, or traumas. These couples might have a temporary experience in the third cycle before they return to any one of the other cycles. The fourth cycle of love and resilience can come after a period of disharmony or conflict and be short-lived before a couple returns to any one of the other cycles.

A Mindful Loving relationship is an entity and grows and develops over time much like the growth and development of each human being. Understanding the various Cycles of Mindful Loving helps us make sense of the many changes we experience in the life of our loving relationships. It is normal and necessary for us to go through changes in our loving relationships.

Mindful Loving takes courage as we lean in toward each other and sustain connection through the challenges of change. Mindful Loving is a place to call home - a place where we experience the natural elements of joy, fear, sadness, and anger.

Just as a child needs a healthy, safe, and secure environment to complete developmental milestones, a couple needs to create a supportive, loving, and respectful environment to navigate through the Cycles of Mindful Loving. Through the course of these cycles, we create a safe and secure base from which to venture forward. Our individual growth and development contribute to our resilience and the celebration of our strength and prepares us for each growth cycle.

Read the Cycles of Mindful Loving, and be aware of the lessons you have already experienced as well as the lessons you will experience throughout the Cycles of Mindful Loving.

The First Cycle of Mindful Loving

The First cycle of is characterized by love and attraction. It is like springtime. We enter new or renewing love. In this cycle, new love occurs when we experience a sense of passion, exhilaration, and the feeling of "falling in love." This is where the foundation of Loving Communication begins as we open ourselves and our hearts to a loving connection with another person. We rearrange our lives and reprioritize our time to cultivate the exciting new relationship. We feel a sense of excitement and anticipation. In new love, our romantic partner is at the center of our world and we begin imagining how the relationship can fulfill our deepest purpose and passion.

Research shows there are neurochemical changes in our brains in the initial stages of a new love relationship. Our brains begin to be flooded with neurochemicals that contribute to feelings of happiness, euphoria, and an intense attraction to our new love. In this euphoria, we can experience an addiction-like obsession to our new partner. These neurochemicals hijack our brains, and we become driven by a constant desire for connection.

As an example, consider the following:

> When Yvette and Claude entered the first cycle of their Mindful Loving relationship they were constantly calling, texting, and rearranging their schedules to spend time together. It was as though they couldn't get enough of each other. This time of passion allowed them to open their hearts, feel safe with one another, and build a foundation for love and intimate connection. They each felt a strong attraction to the other and took emotional risks that felt intoxicating.

We develop a positive illusion of our partners perceiving all that is good and editing out flaws or red flags. During this time, we might overlook differences that can present challenges in future cycles of our Mindful Loving relationships.

Attraction is a key component of this cycle for new and renewing love. Attraction is about both feeling attractive and being attracted to your partner. The attraction template in the brain serves to fine-tune the types of people to whom you are attracted. This helps you narrow the playing field of potential partners. Attraction includes physical, mental, emotional, sexual, and spiritual attractions.

Attraction alone cannot sustain a Mindful Loving relationship; attraction is only a doorway to deeper Mindful Loving.

Physical attraction can be a dominating feature in new love relationships and is shaped by our culture, social norms, and expectations.

Consider the following scenario:

> When Carlos and Bianca met, they had an immediate physical attraction to each other. Bianca was slender and physically fit and had a contagious laugh. Carlos was also physically fit and had beautiful deep brown eyes that contributed to his mysterious allure.
>
> Their physical attraction to each other led to a sexual attraction, creating an addiction-like euphoria and leaving them wanting to spend all their time with each other. The energy between them was electric. Their ensuing sexual relationship was wild and passionate.

Consider the following question: In the beginning of your new love relationship in what ways did you feel love and attraction?

Renewing love involves revisiting the experiences of the First Cycle of Mindful Loving. Renewing love can occur at any time and during the lifetime of a Mindful Loving relationship. It is the experience of love, attraction, and purpose that comes from a deeper connection with each other. As a result of sharing our lives, we look at each other with greater knowing, acceptance, and respect. Experiencing the realities of life helps weather times of disconnection, complacency, and conflict. This deeper connection with each other leads to a resurgence of our passion, love, and attraction for one another, we can feel as if we are falling in love all over again.

Renewing love rekindles connection, engagement, and attraction. In this cycle of renewing love, we enhance physical, mental, emotional, sexual, and spiritual intimacy.

Tyler and Wendy are examples of renewing love:

> Throughout their marriage, Tyler and Wendy practiced Loving Communication skills. They shared many joyful experiences with the celebration of their growing family as well as meeting challenges of career changes and financial stresses. Mindful Loving helped them keep their relationship on track and supported their individual as well as relationship growth. For their tenth wedding anniversary, Tyler and Wendy decided to take a second honeymoon and renew their vows.

> Their renewed vows reflected their enhanced love and attraction:

> > "We commit to understand and respect each other."
> > "We prioritize time, attention, and care for each other."
> > "We use the basic components of Mindful Loving every day."

Physical and sexual attraction grows as a Mindful Loving relationship grows and matures. Our attraction to our partners can become deeper, richer, and more erotic than ever in this cycle of renewing love.

Consider the following example:

> Throughout the course of their marriage, Bonnie and Joe used the basic components of Mindful Loving. They faced challenges that provided many opportunities to practice Loving Communication and Understanding & Respecting Differences. After forty years of marriage, they were still physically and sexually attracted to each other. Joe still looked at Bonnie with desire and a twinkle in his eye, and he told her she was even sexier than ever. Bonnie was

filled with love and contentment. Often, she would smile coyly, take his hand, and lead him into the bedroom.

As they each grew and changed over the years, they regularly shared differing needs and desires. Bonnie expressed a desire for increased touch and tenderness while Joe wanted more time and attention to their lovemaking. Their sexual relationship blossomed as they developed a rich repertoire of tender and exciting lovemaking and thoroughly enjoyed their sexual encounters.

Consider the following question: As you and your partner have grown and changed, how have you continued to express love and attraction for each other?

This First Cycle of Mindful Loving is a time of love and attraction. We build a solid foundation when we practice the basics of Mindful Loving: Loving Communication and Understanding & Respecting Differences.

It is a time when we risk being vulnerable and allow our partners to see the depth of who we really are. Mindful Loving offers us the opportunity to share the truth about ourselves – the good, the bad, the ugly, and the beautiful. In renewing love, we experience the challenges of our differences and make conscious decisions to stay open to the growth and development of ourselves and our relationships.

We learn to love with an open heart and stay curious about each other and ourselves. In this cycle, two individuals develop a new identity as a loving couple. Experiencing such intimate connection with another can be terrifying and exhilarating at the same time!

The Second Cycle of Mindful Loving

The Second Cycle of Mindful Loving is characterized by love and acceptance. It is like summertime. The newness of the relationship wanes, and the roots of our love grow deeper. It is a time of discovery, and it challenges partners to evaluate what works and what needs to change for Mindful Loving to thrive and grow. In this cycle, we utilize the basic components of Mindful Loving, Loving Communication, and Understanding & Respecting Differences more intentionally. We continue to take greater emotional risks and manage our vulnerability. This produces a passion that is a more vibrant expression of our love and connection.

The Second Cycle of Mindful Loving is a cycle of growth. We move from falling in love to being in love, experiencing heightened levels of love and passion. We begin to expand our own identities and sense of purpose as individuals and as a loving couple. This cycle is marked by greater discovery, self-acceptance, and vulnerability. In this cycle, we continue to take emotional risks and are more honest with each other and ourselves. This strengthens our emotional connection.

Growth is first and foremost an individual process. Each partner grows and adds new dimensions to the relationship. Growing puts us in a state of imbalance. When a toddler is learning to walk, he stands; he teeters and often falls as he develops his new walking skills. Sometimes he will reach out for a hand to gain more confidence as he takes his first steps.

For a child, reaching for support is another level of building trust.

In Mindful Loving, we also teeter and fall as we experience the natural changes of our growth and development. It is a time when we live the nuts and bolts of daily life together. We experience the addition of children, changes in careers, education, relocation, blending families, health challenges, and increases in financial responsibilities. We can experience emotional changes ranging from feeling connected to feeling disconnected, from feeling comfort to feeling discomfort, from feeling loved to feeling neglected, and from feeling secure to feeling stuck.

In the Second Cycle of Mindful Loving, we learn to become each other's Go-To Person and reach out for each other to gain confidence and stability.

Being out of balance is a natural and temporary consequence of growth. During this second cycle of love and acceptance, we need to be mindful and give extra attention to ourselves and each other to regain balance.

During this Second Cycle of Mindful Loving, we experience changes in our relationships. Some of these changes involve the integration of the neurochemical influences that hijacked our brains in the First Cycle of Mindful Loving. This is a normal and healthy rebalancing that takes place in the second cycle of our Mindful Loving relationships. Many of the joys, ease, and spontaneity experienced in the first cycle of love and attraction now seem to have changed. Some of these changes include changes in our sexual relationships, decreased time for each other, and increases in responsibilities. We can get caught up in the work of our lives and lose touch with joy and relaxation. Seriousness can plague our lives. This is a time when we need to consciously put fun and play into our lives. When we remember to lighten up, we nurture the capacity to truly engage in and enjoy each other.

In this Second Cycle of Mindful Loving, we learn to become more proactive. When we are proactive, we are less inclined to be reactive. Reactivity is an unconscious pattern of behavior that is repetitive and driven by habit. Being proactive is a mindful practice that enables us to be present and engage in authentic and purposeful interactions.

Consider the following scenario:

> Patrick and Heather were experiencing changes in their sexual relationship. Patrick expressed his frustration and complained that Heather was always tired and never wanted to have sex. Heather was sad about the changes in their sex life but felt overwhelmed by the demands of her life. Sex had become a chore and not the pleasure she had experienced before having children.

Instead of allowing resentment and guilt to build, they were proactive and agreed to have a Loving Communication conversation. Patrick initiated with an "I" Message: "Heather, I love you and I miss you. Whenever we do have sex, it feels like you are a million miles away and just going through the motions. I know you love me and feel frustrated about the change in our sex life and I want to find a way to fix this."

Although initially reactive and defensive, Heather stopped and took some deep breathes. She decided to practice the skill of Listen from the Heart to Understand. She heard Patrick's love for her, and it allowed her to feel vulnerable and express her sadness. She admitted that sex had become a chore and not a priority. Her struggle with the stress in her life made it difficult for her to stay present and enjoy sex.

Because of her openness and vulnerability, Patrick was able to understand and respect the changes and her struggles with sex. They both agreed their sex life was important. They continued their Loving Communication and were proactive in creating a new plan to spice up their sex life. This new commitment led to greater understanding, fun, and intimacy for both of them.

Without care and attention to changes we feel in the relationship, there is a greater risk of developing feelings of guilt and resentment over the demands and challenges of daily life. These demands can create distractions and chaos that get in the way of attending to our relationship and the things that are most important in our lives. When we stay mindful of the impact of these demands and remember to care and nurture ourselves and each other, we then experience the deepening of our passion and purpose. Mindful Loving helps us prioritize the most important things in our lives.

Consider the following example:

Ashley and Mario felt as if their lives were out of control. They had been married for five years after blending their two families. Ashley had two boys, ages nine and seven. Mario had a fifteen-year-old girl and a thirteen-year-old boy. As a family, they developed an acceptable schedule for shared custody. They put conscious effort into managing all the changes that came with blending their families.

Mario's job was demanding and required out-of-town travel, which left Ashley managing the daily routine in the household along with carpooling the children to their music lessons, soccer practices, and other activities. Some days Mario and Ashley did not see each other at all, other days they would only saw each other in passing. They both missed each other and realized they needed to prioritize time for each other.

During one of their weekly dates, their Loving Communication helped them talk about their feelings of disconnection. They discovered that it was not only their crazy schedules and time apart but also their use of technology when they were together that contributed to the imbalance and sense of disconnection. They agreed to modify their use of technology and be more mindful of prioritizing each other. They agreed to talk every evening before going to bed instead of being on their phones. This helped them solidify their emotional connection.

This Second Cycle of Mindful Loving is marked by the need to prioritize time for tender and tough conversations. During this cycle of love and acceptance, we learn to identify our needs; set boundaries; and create time for selves, each other, and family. It is not easy to juggle the many roles and responsibilities in our lives. As we grow and adapt, we must make conscious decisions about how to live and love mindfully.

Consider the following scenario:

Colleen and Mark were actively involved in their careers, church, and in their fifteen-year-old twin daughters' many activities. Evenings and weekends were filled with carpooling and attending practices, games, and recitals.

Mark began feeling overwhelmed and detached from Colleen. Their busy schedule resulted in less time and connection in their marriage. Even though Colleen felt exhausted at times, she believed it was a normal result of a family with two active teenage daughters.

Neither Mark nor Colleen discussed their feelings until they had a huge fight. Mark shared his frustration by blaming Colleen and her over investment with the girls, which left her fatigued and disinterested in him or their relationship. He complained about the lack of sex and said he missed free time for himself and alone time with Colleen.

Colleen reacted with defensiveness. She accused him of not valuing her commitment to providing a rich and exciting life for their daughters. She was torn by the expectations of being a good mother and her role as a good wife.

Over the course of many tough and honest conversations, both Colleen and Mark were able to express hurts, unmet needs, and desires for change. Mark discovered that he felt pressure to be a super dad which overshadowed his enjoyment of his girls and their activities. Colleen discovered that she had neglected her own self-care as well as her needs as a wife in order to be a supermom.

Together they realized it was not helpful for them to ignore their own needs for fun and connection or to be so child-centered. It was as important for them to prioritize time with each other as it was to prioritize time with the girls. They recognized that these changes also modeled important lessons about Mindful Loving for their daughters. They understood that the purpose of this conflict led them to greater intimacy, acceptance, and love for each other.

Consider the following question: In what ways do you prioritize time for tender and tough conversations?

An important skill in the Second Cycle of Mindful Loving is being present in the moment. To be present means we consciously pay attention to the moment and tune in with all our senses. Being present allows us to let go of all the extraneous distractions. This practice contributes to feeling emotionally connected and validated.

When we are not being present, we are not fully listening and remembering the things that our partners are saying. How many times do you have conversations while texting or looking at your phone? Contrary to popular belief, we cannot multitask and maintain the same level of attention we display when we are absolutely present.

> Have you ever had the experience of talking to your partner and feeling as if he or she is not paying attention? It can be hurtful or irritating when your partner appears to be listening but is not really present.

> Have you ever had the experience of not being present when your partner is talking to you, when you look as if you are giving your attention while doing or thinking about something else? Even if you think you listened, by not being fully present in the moment, you missed something from the interaction.

Most of us have gotten into the habit of not being present in the moment during most of our day. Even though we are dedicated and committed to our partners, it is easy to become complacent and even lazy about being present with our partners. The good news is that we can change the habit and start being more present for our partners and our own lives right now!

In the Second Cycle of Mindful Loving, our differences and limitations are more readily noticed and recognized. Couples begin seeing each other more clearly without the rose-colored glasses. This is a time when we grow to love and accept our partners for who they really are, not who we want them to be.

Many people want the fantasy of living happily ever after and believe that when we truly love someone, it should be easy. This fantasy is nurtured by romance novels, fairy tales, and Hollywood movies and can give us an unrealistic sense of what a loving relationship looks like. Measuring our relationships to the living happily ever after fantasy, contributes to disappointments and dissatisfaction in our real-life relationships. It can be a time when our thoughts turn complaints, such as the following:

> "Our relationship is not fun anymore."
> "You're not the same person I fell in love with."
> "We don't spend time with each other like we used to."
> "I feel like we are not in love anymore".

These thoughts are warning signals. When we neglect to pay attention to these warning signals, we miss the opportunity to heal and revitalize our relationships.

Conflicts and disagreements naturally arise in every relationship. It's not the conflicts, but how we handle them that is important. When manage conflicts with respect and acceptance, they create greater emotional intimacy and connection. When we use blame, criticism, and anger to deal with conflicts, those conflicts threaten our sense of security. Criticism and blame are reactive patterns and have toxic effects on a relationship.

Sometimes couples resort to defensiveness and criticism to deal with conflict and differences. These practices can be damaging and threaten the stability of the relationship. Instead, the continued practice of the basic components of Mindful Loving helps us move forward to a more loving, respectful, and intimate relationships. The decision to love and be loving contributes to building love and acceptance in our relationships.

Consider the following example:

> Anna and Keagan were learning to take responsibility for themselves and the way in which some of their old communication patterns had been destructive in their relationship. Keagan was learning to manage his criticisms and quick temper when he felt ignored. Anna was learning to express her feelings without defensiveness when she felt hurt.

When Anna got a new phone, she asked Keagan to show her how to use it. Keagan started explaining about all the exciting new functions of the phone. Anna listened and began feeling overwhelmed with all the information. She interrupted him, saying, "Just tell me what to do and how to use it."

Keagan became frustrated with Anna's interruptions. He raised his voice and criticized her for not wanting to learn about her new phone. Anna became defensive and upset that Keagan was getting angry and not listening to what she wanted. In her frustration, she yelled, "Just forget it, I'll do it myself!" and she retreated to the bedroom in tears.

After a ten-minute time-out, she returned, apologized and suggested they have a Do-Over. When she reflected on her part in the exchange, Anna realized she had fallen into her old patterns of running away when she felt hurt and overwhelmed.

Keagan thanked her for coming back to talk. During his ten-minute time-out, he'd examined his part in what had just happened. He apologized for the way he'd handled his frustration: by getting angry and criticizing her. He realized he just wanted to help her but was giving her information she didn't really want or need.

They both recognized that in the past, this kind of argument would have resulted in a disconnection with each spending hours or days feeling hurt and angry.

They were grateful for how they both had taken responsibility for their own experiences. By hanging in there during times of minor challenges, they resolved the conflict more effectively. They continued to grow and strengthen their love and resilience.

Gratitude and expressions of appreciation are the mainstays of Mindful Loving. Gratitude involves choosing to focus on the positive and appreciate what is good in life. A Mindful Loving relationship requires nurturing and care. The high divorce rate and the increasing number of couples living in unhappy or unhealthy relationships are signals that relationships need to use the basic components of Mindful Loving and Practical Tools. In the First Cycle of Mindful Loving, you typically put a lot of time, attention, and care into the relationship. Once you make a commitment, get married and settle into life together, the amount of quality time, attention, and energy often decreases. Many couples complain that life gets in the way of maintaining a healthy connection and attention to each other. Often, couples begin to prioritize other things, such as work, children, and school, and begin to operate from the squeaky-wheel principle: who or whatever squeaks the loudest or puts the greatest demand gets the attention.

Consider the following questions:

>**Who or what is "squeaking" in your relationship?**
>**What are the things that might be taking your attention away from gratitude and appreciation?**

Even on the worst days, we have the option to acknowledge and express gratitude and appreciation for the smallest things in our lives.

Being present in the moment enables us to be proactive instead of reactive. When we are proactive, we first become aware of our experience and acknowledge what is going on. Being proactive enables us to pay attention and then create a plan to make things different.

Consider the following example:

>Jorge is an accountant who spends four months out of the year buried in his work. He and his wife, Lidia, plan a romantic weekend getaway before his busy season and a vacation week after the season to prioritize their relationship.

>Jorge and Lidia are proactive in planning time together to prevent potential disconnection in their relationship during the busy tax season. Proactivity enables them to stay focused on what is most important before they encounter major problems.

Being present in the moment and proactive breaks the chain of reactivity and allows us to control our responses to life. It empowers us to grow and be free to be our best selves. Consider the following example:

> Jarrod and Beverly started fighting about household chores. Beverly felt overwhelmed in trying to manage the household chores and the stresses of her job. Jarrod complained and criticized when the house was a mess or the laundry wasn't done. Beverly reacted with anger and blamed Jarrod for not being more helpful and understanding. Criticism and blame began to erode their connection.

> Their fight escalated when they were preparing for a visit from Jarrod's parents. Beverly finally blew up and yelled at Jarrod for being inconsiderate and unsupportive. Jarrod was defensive and confused about Beverly's comments. After several minutes of slinging blame and accusations at each other, Jarrod suggested that they stop the fighting.

> They agreed they wanted to stop the fighting. Beverly shared that what she really wanted was for Jarrod to help out more with the household chores. She told him that his criticisms were hurtful. While listening to Beverly, Jarrod began to understand how his criticism was eroding their connection and care for each other. They agreed to produce a new schedule for household chores.

> They acknowledged that the purpose of their fight was not just about the chores but also about how they were disrespecting each other. They realized that it only took one of them to suggest they stop fighting before they were able to move into a constructive resolution.

During this cycle of love and acceptance, couples challenged in the relationship. Sometimes one partner is doing all the work to keep the relationship together and can end up feeling depleted and frustrated. This can result in disconnection and feelings of resentment. When we are disconnected, we attach to old practices, perceptions, and reactions.

When disconnection occurs, we always have a choice: we can either continue building a stronger foundation or continue enduring the pattern of disconnection.

Mindful Loving helps us meet these challenges. These challenges are as natural as the summer storms that roll in. In this cycle of love and acceptance, we experience a fundamentally deeper level of connection and intimacy. When we stay conscious of Mindful Loving practices, we make choices about how to nurture ourselves, our partners, and our relationships. Mindful Loving becomes a decision every day to love and be loved.

The Third Cycle of Mindful Loving

The Third Cycle of Mindful Loving is characterized by love and transition. It is like the fall season in nature. Fall is a reminder that there are natural transitions - nothing stays the same. It is time for harvesting and managing the various transitions in life.

Transitions are a natural part of life. Transitions signify movement in our lives – a passage from one state to another. As we transition into this cycle of Mindful Loving, we experience both celebrations and losses. We celebrate graduations, marriages, grandchildren, career recognitions, advancements, and other changes. We experience losses, such as deaths of friends and family, children leaving, and downsizing our home or lifestyle. Many of us transition to caretaking roles for our aging parents. We all are affected by the physical and emotional changes in our own health, bodies, and lifestyle.

During this cycle, our meaningful reflections prompt us to explore where we are in our lives, in our jobs, careers, and in our love relationships. It is a time for examining and redefining our own sense of purpose. The continued practice of Mindful Loving helps us move through these transitions. It is a time when we deepen our love and connection by continuing to practice the basics of Mindful Loving. This Third Cycle of Mindful Loving is a time of minor and major transitions. All transitions require some degree of adaptation.

Minor transitions can occur on a repeating cycle, like the end of summer vacation and the start of the school year, preparation for holidays, vacations, and other times of celebration. Minor transitions can also be the result of an unexpected event in our lives, such as the sudden loss of a job or a move.

Consider the following example:

> After five years of marriage, Jamel and Leila faced an unexpected transition. Jamel lost his job and was not able to find work. At the same time, Leila was offered a promotion that required relocation. They faced this challenge together and re-examined their priorities.

They decided that Leila would accept the promotion. This decision meant they would be leaving the familiarity of family and friends.

Jamel felt a sense of failure in not being able to secure employment. He'd grew up believing his purpose and role was to be the primary breadwinner in his family. He and Leila had decided that his being the provider would enable Leila to stay home when they started their family. Leila felt conflicted because she was excited about her new position, but it meant delaying their plans of starting a family.

Together they constructed a new plan for their lives. The job loss allowed Jamal to reshape his career goals. He and Leila agreed that Leila would support the family as Jamal developed his own business. Instead of this challenge being a negative event in their lives, Leila and Jamal used it as an opportunity to grow. The challenge became a catalyst for redefining their roles and expectations. Their entire decision-making process served to deepen their love connection.

Through the practice of Loving Communication, they stayed open and curious about their options and shared their hopes and fears about their new life adventure. Their conversations helped them Understand & Respect Differences as they considered the impact of the move.

Major transitions occur over time, such as the physical and hormonal changes we experience in mid-life. Other major transitions occur with retirement, career changes, health challenges, the death of a loved one, or changes in our family life. Major life transitions provide us with an opportunity to reorganize and restructure our lives. These life transitions challenge us to examine our lives and relationships.

For some parents, it is a welcomed blessing and celebration when their children leave home and are launched into adulthood. For other parents, children leaving home can be an exceedingly difficult transition. These parents often have prioritized their role as parents, sometimes at the expense of prioritizing their love relationship. These parents can have greater difficulty with the grieving process of letting go and transitioning to the next stage of family life.

Consider the following example:

> Barry and Jenn have been married for twenty-three years. Their demanding jobs and focus on their only daughter's life and activities consumed much of their time and attention. When their daughter left for college, they found themselves alone together with a quiet discomfort. There was a deep feeling of disconnection. They had nothing to talk about and felt that they barely knew each other anymore outside the context of parenting their daughter.
>
> One day, Jenn overheard Barry talking to a friend about his new found passion for meditations and spirituality. She realized she'd had no idea he was so interested in spirituality. At first, she felt angry and excluded from his life. She later recognized that her anger was really about the sadness she felt from being so estranged from his new sense of passion and purpose. She wondered if he knew how much she enjoyed learning about her newfound passion for nutrition and exercise.
>
> She felt nervous but asked Barry if they could talk. She told him about her sadness. "We've been so busy with other parts of our lives that we have lost touch with each other, and it feels like we don't even know each other anymore. I love you and want us to be friends again."
>
> Barry had been feeling a sense of disconnection as well. He told Jenn he appreciated her courage in starting the conversation.

The journey of rekindling passion and purpose begins when both partners are willing to be vulnerable and honest about their feelings. They must be vulnerable enough to risk examining and restructuring their relationship. This is not an easy task. The practice of Listening from the Heart to Understand results in deeper loving and greater intimacy.

Barry and Jenn took the risk and committed time and attention to their process of reconnection and restructuring their relationship. They scheduled weekly conversations about how to live their lives from a healthier and more spiritual place. Together they explored educational opportunities and went to self-growth, yoga, and meditation retreats. They consciously reimagined their lives, which helped rekindle the passion and purpose in their Mindful Loving relationship.

The Third Cycle of Mindful Loving is a time when we are confronted with choices; it is a time for reflection and transformation. Prioritizing and giving care and attention to our relationships helps us move through what can often be a challenging time. This cycle is also a time for recognizing and celebrating the milestones and accomplishments in our lives.

When we embrace new practices, as demonstrated by Barry and Jenn, we continue to grow and enhance our lives and our relationships. Many couples find new ways to prioritize their relationships and create new rituals for maintaining growth and connection through transitions.

Another major transition is dealing with health challenges. We might not always have a choice about what happens to us, but we have a choice about how to deal with it.

Consider the following scenario:

Nick and Kristina had been married for ten years when Kristina was diagnosed with breast cancer. They cried together and shared their fears of the unknown. They faced many months of intense stress in dealing with the diagnosis and treatment of her breast cancer.

Kristina was able to talk about the overwhelming range of feelings she experienced. She shared her fear of dying. She questioned her ability to withstand the pain and horror of surgery and chemotherapy treatments. She expressed fear that a mastectomy would cause changes in her body and her worry that Nick would no longer find her attractive.

Nick listened from his heart and provided Kristina with reassurance and comfort. After the initial shock, he accepted his primary role as her Go-To Person. He served as her advocate in dealing with the frustrating maze of insurance and medical services. He was her caregiver and protected her from any additional stress. It was not until the end of her treatments that Nick was able to express the depth of his own feelings. Through Loving Communication, he shared how scared he was of losing her, the love of his life.

The many months of Kristina's health struggles stressed each of them in separate ways. Through their Mindful Loving, they stayed connected and grew closer and more intimate. As they celebrated the completion of her treatment, they were proud of their ability to weather such a major transition.

Midlife is a major transition, as we move through physical, social, and psychological changes. We can choose to experience a midlife crisis, or we can choose midlife renewal.

Sometimes this major transition can feel overwhelming. We can feel depressed when we have thoughts like the following:

> *Half of my life is over, and what do I have to show for it?*
> *The changes in my appearance make me feel invisible.*
> *I am feeling displaced by the push from the next generation and*
> *overwhelmed by technological advances.*

These types of thoughts lead to feelings of anxiety, sadness, and resignation. We have a choice in dealing with these feelings.

Self-reflection is critical in dealing with mid-life transition.

Honest self-examination gives us insight and the ability to make healthy choices. Without this first step, many of us try to grab happiness and make changes to the outside of our lives. We quit jobs, leave marriages, buy new sports cars, or have affairs, seeking quick fixes to the feelings that accompany our midlife transitions.

Choosing self-reflection first enables us to go inward and accept all the feelings we are having. It is natural to feel anxiety and sadness when we go through major life changes. The difference between midlife crisis and midlife renewal is that, in midlife renewal, we use these feelings as a springboard for growth and enhancement instead of feeling stuck, lost, or depressed. We begin to replace old thoughts with new ones:

> *I am grateful for all the experiences I have had and am excited to expand and share my wisdom with others.*
> *I am redefining my sense of beauty and power.*
> *I embrace technology and value its use in my life.*

We have a choice to replace old, unhealthy thoughts. This requires us to take personal responsibility for how we are thinking and make a conscious decision to change our thoughts. Reorganizing and restructuring our thinking helps us experience our best selves and prepares us for a rich second half of life.

Making changes from the inside can lead us to midlife renewal. Some decisions we make might include re-evaluating our job and careers, enhancing our marriages, improving our health and fitness, and finding new communities of support as we look forward to the adventures of the second half of life.

Staying open to natural changes in our lives and our relationships helps us make transitions with greater ease. In this third cycle, that we become more active and responsible for creating the new direction in our lives and in our relationships.

Consider the following example:

> Paul and Abbey had moved through many minor and major transitions in their twenty year marriage. As they reflected on

their life together, they were proud of their accomplishments and how they had managed the many transitions.

Their oldest daughter left for college, Paul's mother passed away, and they moved Abbey's father into a memory-care facility. Abbey changed careers, leaving twenty years of teaching to open her new art studio. Paul's promotion at work created more financial security for the family which also placed additional demands on his time and energy.

They used many tools to help them stay connected and manage the many transitions in their life:

- They scheduled and prioritized time together.
- They used Loving Communication and had Big-Talk conversations.
- They scheduled time for fun, play, and relaxation.
- They scheduled regular dates and explored new experiences together.
- They committed to daily expressions of appreciation and gratitude.

These practices helped Paul and Abbey manage the difficult challenges they faced with their parents. Committing to Loving Communication enabled Abbey to acknowledge her desire for a career change. This helped Paul support her and be her Go-To-Person as she faced her decision. Their commitment to Mindful Loving during this third cycle helped them enrich their individual lives and their relationship which contributed to their midlife renewal.

There is a natural imbalance every time we experience transitions. Think about a tightrope walker who must rebalance with every step he takes to move forward. Every time we experience transition, we also experience moments of imbalance before we re-stabilize. By accepting the natural process of transition and change, we are better able to move forward through our transitions.

Ignoring or resisting these natural changes only serves to contribute to the midlife crisis. Fear and resistance to these inevitable changes can lead to turmoil and stagnation and stunt our growth. Resisting change inhibits our ability to weather transitions.

Resistance to change is characterized by not prioritizing time for self-care and self-reflection, which results in our emotional lives spinning out of control. This creates chronic stress, emotional imbalance, and unhappiness. It can become easy to blame and criticize our partners as the source of our unhappiness instead of recognizing that our own discontent and unhappiness are within us. This can result in angry explosions or destructive withdrawals, which harm our emotional connections with those we love the most. Some partners become defensive or shut down, turning on each other instead of turning toward each other to explore their emotional needs.

Consider the following example:

> On the outside, it appeared that Peter and Cara were a happy and successful couple. On the inside, however, they were both unhappy and struggling in their marriage.
>
> Cara felt lonely in her marriage. She found herself attracted to and emotionally involved with a male coworker. Cara began talking with him and shared intimate details of her life. She talked about her loneliness and unhappiness. Her coworker listened and seemed genuinely interested, which made her feel valued and important. When she was sitting at home with Peter, she realized that she was missing this kind of emotional connection with her own husband. As her confusion and discomfort grew, she became overwhelmed and did not know what to do with these feelings.
>
> Cara began by telling Peter she was unhappy in the marriage. She complained about his lack of attention and interest in her and even accused him of having an affair. She proceeded with a laundry list of complaints. She was angry about having to do everything from managing the house and the finances to maintaining their

social life. She did not feel his support when she took care of his disabled mother or their grandchildren. She blamed him for her unhappiness.

Peter felt blindsided and reacted with anger. He vehemently denied having an affair and criticized Cara for her sexual rejections, moodiness and weight gain and acting like a martyr. Once he said it aloud, there was no going back, and Peter became aware of his own unhappiness.

They hit a marital crisis and were stuck in old patterns. They each only saw what was wrong with the other. They were not able to recognize or take responsibility for their own part in contributing to the crisis. They struggled to find what was right or what they loved about each other. Neither of them knew what to do to move forward and close the emotional gap. They decided to seek professional help.

We need to continue using the basic components of Mindful Loving throughout the Cycles of Mindful Loving. As we weather transitions, we look at each other with either sadness and regret or with love and appreciation. Mindful Loving helps us manage transitions and challenges in our lives and in our relationships.

Transitions are inevitable. Hurt, disappointment, and disconnection are natural experiences in life. There are times when couples have done the best they can to work through the difficulties in their relationship and decide to end the relationship.

It is how we handle challenges that is most important. The continued practice of self-care, Loving Communication, and Understanding & Respecting Differences helps us move through this cycle with greater ease. It contributes to the renewal of our passion and purpose.

It is important to seek professional help when necessary. This is a sign of strength and commitment to a Mindful Loving relationship.

The Fourth Cycle of Mindful Loving

The Fourth Cycle of Mindful Loving is characterized by love and resilience. It is like the winter season in nature, when trees lose their leaves, providing a new view of their strength and vitality. Plants seem to disappear, yet their roots are still alive beneath the surface.

In this Cycle of Mindful Loving, mature love grows into a deep, enduring, and solid connection. This cycle offers the quiet comfort we feel after a delightful shared experience or the calm that follows a challenge managed with love and respect.

Resilience is the inner strength that helps us bounce back from challenges or challenging times. As individuals, it gives us a sense of purpose and a clarity of our values. As a couple, resilience helps us keep our hearts open to giving and receiving love throughout the course of our Mindful Loving relationships.

This Cycle of Mindful Loving is a time of reflection and reconnection. It presents the opportunity to move inward. In nature, trees lose their leaves and pull their energy inward. This helps them manage the harsher winter elements and prepare for the new growth of spring. We too, need to move inward as we deal with challenges and prepare for our new growth. During this time, it is important to accept and take responsibility for our own experiences, dreams, and desires.

For some couples, it is a time when they recognize their accomplishments and prepare to redesign the next stage of their lives to fulfill their dreams and desires.

Consider this example:

> Jason and Gloria both enjoyed good health and led active lives. They felt accomplished in fulfilling their earlier life purpose of creating a healthy and happy family and career lives. Retirement gave them the opportunity to explore how they wanted to reimagine and redefine their purpose for this next stage in their lives. They

had many conversations about their options. They thought about moving closer to their children and grandchildren, downsizing to a smaller home, or moving into an active adult community.

The decision to move to an active adult community was in alignment with their passion for expanding their social community, enjoying activities, and cultivating new interests. Their new purpose was to be grateful and to focus on simplifying and enjoying their life. They loved thinking about this stage in their lives as "refirement", a time to re-fire their lives and their love, instead of retiring from their lives.

For some couples who experience disconnection and feel the chill of resentments, this cycle provides the opportunity to evaluate the viability of the relationship. It is either the wake-up call for reconnection or the beginning of dissolution. In these times, couples might seek professional help.

As an example, remember Cara and Peter who chose marital therapy.

Cara and Peter chose marital therapy to do the work for reconnection. Through her work in marital therapy, Cara acknowledged her unhappiness and admitted that she had not been taking good care of herself. She complained about her hormonal imbalances and feeling tired and unattractive. Cara had blamed Peter for her unhappiness and expected him to fix it.

Her work in therapy helped her commit to prioritizing her self-care. She became more willing to take responsibility for her own happiness and re-evaluated her unrealistic expectations of Peter. This freed her from the burden of her resentments and allowed her to accept and forgive Peter. She realized the conversations with and attractions for her co-worker were not healthy for her and decided to end that relationship.

Through his work in therapy, Peter recognized his resentments and realized he blamed Cara for the emotional distance he felt in their marriage. Peter acknowledged that he had allowed his work to fill all his emotional needs. He had become complacent in the marriage and stopped communicating and sharing with Cara. In therapy, he learned Loving Communications skills. By using these new skills, he talked more openly and honestly.

They developed a plan to reconnect and heal their relationship:

- They reaffirmed their love for each other.
- They prioritized self-care.
- They learned and used the basics of Mindful Loving: Loving Communication and Understanding & Respecting Differences.

As they both shared their more vulnerable feelings of disconnection and despair, they began to understand each other in new ways. They saw how blame and criticism had hurt their relationship, and both regretted the wasted years of living with such unhappiness.

Each took responsibility and apologized for his or her part in hurting the other. They learned the practice of acceptance and forgiveness. Even though they had experienced the chill of disconnection, their love and resilience allowed them to do the work necessary to heal their relationship.

Cara and Peter demonstrated resilience and healing by rebuilding love for each other. As with remodeling a home, we must first create a plan of what we want and what needs to change. Sometimes we just need to repaint the walls or change the flooring. Other times we need to remove walls and take the house down to the studs to reconstruct and transform the home.

Resilience is the ability to manage daily stresses. The two most important practices that strengthen resilience are the following:

- Acceptance
- Forgiveness

Acceptance is a process in which we first recognize what is. We then own our own experience, thoughts, and feelings and, finally, accept them without judgment. When our judgments of ourselves or our partners lead to blame and criticism, we get stuck and have difficulty moving forward. Resilience helps us move forward.

Forgiveness is a letting-go process that sets us free to love and understand ourselves and our partners more deeply. Forgiveness is an individual experience when we let go of the negative burdens of hurt, fear, resentment, or anger. Forgiveness does not mean accepting damaging behavior or letting ourselves or our partners off the hook. It does mean being free to love ourselves and our partners more fully. Forgiveness is truly a gift we give ourselves. Being resilient in our Mindful Loving becomes a practice of being at peace with ourselves and our partners through acceptance and forgiveness.

This Fourth Cycle of Mindful Loving gives us an opportunity to grow in new ways. The use of the basic components of Mindful Loving helps us navigate our way through minor and major transitions.

An example to consider:

> When Steve retired before Ellen, his retirement caused a major transition in their relationship.
>
> Ellen had always been the one to cook for the family. She would come home after work, change into comfy clothes, and head for the kitchen. Cooking was one of her passions that gave her immense pleasure and helped her unwind from the day.
>
> When Steve retired, he began to take an interest in cooking and discovered he was quite the gourmet cook. He created seafood chowders, whipped up fancy desserts, and discovered a special recipe for marinated scallops. Although Ellen enjoyed his cooking, she felt displaced from her safe spot in the kitchen. She considered it to be her territory and had difficulty relaxing and sharing her turf with Steve.

She became aware of a growing sense of resentment and decided to talk to Steve about her feelings. She told him she appreciated his new culinary interests and contributions. She also told him she relied on cooking as a way for her relax and manage her stress and found the new change difficult.

Steve was surprised that his attempts to be helpful caused distress for Ellen. Through the practice of Loving Communication and Understanding & Respecting Differences, Ellen was able to appreciate Steve's intention to support her, and Steve was able to understand Ellen's feelings and experience with the new change in their routine.

They resolved the challenge and developed a plan to rotate days for each of them to share the cooking. They even spent weekends in the kitchen, experimenting with recipes they prepared together.

Ellen and Steve used the basic components of Mindful Loving, Loving Communication and Understanding & Respecting Differences, to deal with this major transition in their lives.

The Fourth Cycle of Mindful Loving often involves the restructuring of roles and responsibilities in a relationship. The transitions and changes we experience in retirement are good examples of changing roles and routines.

Consider the following example:

For over fifty years, George and Betty had well-established roles and responsibilities in their relationship. They had gotten into comfortable habits of living together. After George retired, he felt lost and uncomfortable when staying home every day. He did not know what to do with himself without having his normal work routine. Betty kept busy with her normal routine of managing the home, volunteering, and gardening.

At first, George followed Betty around, trying to fit into her routine, and gave her suggestions on how to improve her performance.

This drove them both crazy! They realized that their dream of retirement and time together was turning into a nightmare!

They decided to use Loving Communication to talk honestly about their frustrations. During their Loving Communication, George acknowledged his difficulty in adjusting to not having a job to do every day. For the past forty years of his life, he had gone to work in a job that had given him a sense of value and purpose. Now, he was challenged to find a new sense of value and purpose. When George talked to Betty about his struggles, Betty listened from her heart to understand and realized the greater impact of George's retirement.

George and Betty realized they had become set in their ways and had been complacent about their relationship. They decided to restructure their roles and responsibilities. George took over the grocery shopping and Betty started to enjoy working in their new vegetable garden. They planned weekly meals and began cooking together. They structured their days to include time alone balanced with time together. They quickly adapted to their new roles and routines. They felt a renewed partnership emerge as they divided the responsibilities around the home and worked together as a team.

George's retirement and their use of the basic components of Mindful Loving allowed them to reevaluate and restructure their roles. This enabled them to grow into the next level of their Mindful Loving relationship.

When we meet a challenge in our lives with love and respect, we experience resilience and resolution and move on to a deeper connection.

Health challenges, during any cycle, bring up issues of losing a partner or becoming disabled. These are difficult and often frightening life experiences. Love and resilience help us stay strong as we navigate through these challenges.

Consider the following example:

> Tom and Norma were not prepared for the shock and life-altering effects of Tom's sudden heart attack. Norma felt terrified and alone. Tom was her best friend, confidant, and rock. How would she get through this struggle, and even more frightening, how would she go on without him?
>
> Tom had always felt strong and invincible because he had never suffered any health problems and took good care of himself. He began to feel depressed and immobilized by his heart attack. For the first time in his life, he felt his own mortality and fear of death.
>
> This challenge forced them to look at their lives and explore what was most important in their lives now. During the months of recovery and rehabilitation, they had many open and honest conversations. Even though the heart attack was an unexpected challenge, the unexpected gift was the time they spent together rediscovering, redesigning, and rekindling their love and connection.
>
> Norma learned to reach out for the support of family, friends, and a support group for partners of heart attack patients. She also took a leadership role in the family, managing finances, household maintenance, and Tom's rehabilitation schedule. She realized she had a strength and resilience that helped her feel confident and competent.
>
> Tom recognized that it was okay for him to talk about his fears and anxieties and accept help. Through his openness and vulnerability, he discovered an emotional strength he hadn't known he had.
>
> This crisis enriched their love and resilience. They shared a greater sense of appreciation for each other and were grateful for every day they had together.

The death of a partner is a major life-altering experience that can happen in any Cycle of Mindful Loving. It is one of the most difficult challenges we face in our lives. Throughout our Mindful Loving relationships, we face many major and minor transitions with our partners. The death of a partner is a major transition one must face alone. The love and resilience in a Mindful Loving relationship can guide us as we journey through the grieving process.

Consider the following example:

> Ron and Sandy had been married for sixty years when Ron was diagnosed with lung cancer. Over the next five years, they went through multiple treatments until the doctors said there was nothing more they could do. As it became more apparent that Ron was going to die soon, Ron and Sandy spent time talking about their life together and all the things they had cherished sharing.
>
> When they talked about his dying, Ron shared his sadness about leaving Sandy first. He let her know how much he loved her and said he knew she was a strong woman and would be okay.
>
> Sandy experienced the gradual loss of Ron when he no longer reached out to touch her hand and stopped expressing his gratitude for the small acts of service and love she provided for him. She knew he was slowly slipping away, and her world became smaller as they withdrew from usual activities.
>
> Sandy supported Ron's desire to remain home in his final days. With the help of hospice, he enjoyed the familiarity of his home and was surrounded by his family and friends as his life came to an end.
>
> After Ron died, Sandy grieved not only the loss of her partner but also the loss of the dreams and life they'd had together. She felt overwhelmed when she began assuming the responsibilities Ron had managed.

Sandy has a different dream for herself now. She is slowly gaining confidence in managing her life alone. Her Mindful Loving allows her to feel Ron's presence with each step she takes toward her new life without him.

The death of a partner or the loss of a relationship can be an earth-shattering life experience. The pain of loss is profound. Engaging in Mindful Loving sets us up to deal more effectively with the pain of losing our partners. The benefits gained in loving with passion and purpose are gifts that outweigh the fear of pain and loss.

In the Fourth Cycle of Mindful Loving, resilience is the strength that helps us manage and move out of complacency and disconnection. We don't necessarily need a crisis to tap into our resilience. Resilience is the strength that is always present. When Mindful Loving skills are used throughout the Cycles of Mindful Loving, we keep our relationship alive and vibrant.

Understanding the Four Cycles of Mindful Loving

Understanding the four Cycles of Mindful Loving, helps us recognize the characteristics of love, attraction, acceptance, transitions, and resilience. By making conscious decisions to love, we navigate through the Cycles of Mindful Loving and maintain healthy connections. The excitement that is present in the first cycle of love and attraction can still be present in the fourth cycle of love and resilience. As we continue to practice Mindful Loving skills, we cultivate attraction, acceptance, healthy transitioning, and resilience.

In the initial stage of relationships, we are drawn by attraction and usually prioritize our partners over other people and activities. We spend time together in lieu of sleeping, doing chores, or spending time with other friends or family. Over time in our love relationships, we can become complacent and stop dedicating quality time for ourselves and each other. There are natural differences that occur in a Mindful Loving relationship. A lack of understanding and respecting each other can create a disconnection. When we become disconnected from ourselves and each other, we stop being mindful and curious about who and where we are in the present moment. Often, we don't even realize we have stopped feeling joy and excitement about our lives and our relationships. It is as if we are on cruise control without a destination as we move through the many transitions life offers.

It is important to remember that in each Cycle of Mindful Loving, there are unique challenges and opportunities for growth. Our desire for connection, acceptance, and love is fulfilled when we move through the Cycles of Mindful Loving. Our passion and purpose grow and are sustained when we do the work that each cycle offers.

Review the basic components of Mindful Loving- Loving Communication and Understanding & Respecting Differences- and the Cycles of Mindful Loving.

Recognize and acknowledge the work and accomplishments that are already part of your own Mindful Loving relationship, and identify the work to be done.

CHAPTER 3

Practical Tools for Mindful Loving

Being in a Mindful Loving relationship is about being present, intentional, and grateful. Mindful Loving creates a life that is full, open, and joy-filled. A relationship serves as a mirror to reflect and challenge both partners to grow to be their best selves. Mindful Loving is a vehicle that helps you see yourself more clearly as you journey through life together.

Practical Tools are the skills and practices that build, remodel, and strengthen your relationship. Many tools exist, and it is important to find the ones that are exactly right for you. Mindful Loving requires you to re-evaluate, sharpen, and upgrade your practices as you move through the Cycles of Mindful Loving.

The tools that worked at the beginning of your relationship might need upgrading as you and your partner experience life together and meet more complex challenges. Practical Tools provides a menu of resources that guide you through the ongoing growth and development of your Mindful Loving relationship.

We encourage you to read the Practical Tools section and highlight the ones you think will be most helpful for you. Change happens more quickly when you and your partner agree to use these Practical Tools together, so we suggest that you ask your partner to do this as well. Even if your partner is not ready to join you, you can start using these Practical Tools right now. It only takes one partner to implement something new to have a positive impact on the relationship.

Have fun reading all the tools. Choose one tool that will enhance your relationship right now. Commit to implement that tool for a week and see how it goes. After a week, schedule time to talk about the experience.

Here are some questions you can use as part of the conversation:

- How did I feel using this tool?
  Awkward?
  Comfortable?
  Encouraged?
  Did I feel more loving or loved?

- What was my experience when my partner used this tool?
- Did I feel more connected?
- Is this a tool that can become a new practice for us, or do we need to modify it to make it fit better for us?

Take the risk, be proactive, and start with just one Practical Tool to see how you can enhance your Mindful Loving relationship. We purposefully created short, simple practices that can be implemented immediately to experience the rewards of Mindful Loving.

As you use these Practical Tools to enhance your relationship, it is important to remember that the basis of a Mindful Loving relationship is the ability to love yourself first. Make sure you use these Practical Tools to enhance your own self-love as well as your own Mindful Loving relationship.

Practical Tools

1. Be Present and Prioritize Your Mindful Loving Relationship
2. Do and Be Your Best
3. Use "I" Messages
4. Listen from the Heart to Understand
5. Practice Balanced Communication
6. Be Mindful of Your Thoughts
7. Be Mindful of Your Emotions
8. Puke Recycled Emotions
9. Use the 5 to 1 Appreciation Rule
10. Have Daily Big Talk Conversations
11. Have Small Talk and Share Your Day
12. Maintain Contact When You Talk
13. Make Time for Affection
14. Create a Mindful Loving Gratitude Journal
15. Practice Acts of Kindness
16. Lighten Up and Laugh Together (LULT)
17. Play Together
18. Maintain Connection through Writing
19. Schedule Regular Dates with Each Other
20. Schedule Sensual and Sexual Dates
21. Create Your Own Sensual and Sexual Menu
22. Ignite and Maintain Romance
23. Practice Center - Stage Communication
24. Reset the Moment
25. Heal the Hurts in Your Relationship
26. Ask for What You Want and Say What You Don't Want
27. Practice Effective Negotiation
28. Practice Acceptance of Each Other's Differences
29. Manage Communication Differences
30. Use Technology Wisely
31. Be a Life-Long Student of Mindful Loving
32. Create Spiritual Connections
33. Create Your Own Mindful Loving Vision Statement
34. Create and Use Goals to Fulfill Your Mindful Loving Vision
35. Get Professional Help When Needed

1. Be Present and Prioritize Your Mindful Loving Relationship

Being present is a way of living that enables you to experience life more fully. Using this tool means you are present, conscious, and intentional. When you are present, you experience the fullness of the moment. Being present with your partner increases a stronger inner connection.

Some suggestions to help you Be Present with your partner are as follows:

1. Set the intention of being present and attentive to your partner.
2. Stay conscious of when your partner is talking to you, and stop what you are doing so you can give your full attention.
3. If your mind starts to wander, recognize it, take some deep breaths and bring yourself back to the present moment.
4. Use eye contact or touch to reconnect and be present with your partner.

Prioritize Your Mindful Loving Relationship means you set the intention to make your relationship central in your life. You make time to nurture and enjoy each other by making meaningful and loving connections. This helps you keep your relationship alive and vibrant.

Some questions to consider regarding ways you Prioritize Your Mindful Loving Relationship are as follows:

1. Do you still hang out and share activities with each other?
2. Do you laugh and have fun with each other?
3. Do you make time for meaningful sexual connection?
4. Do you still see your partner as your Go-To Person when you are happy, sad, or upset?
5. Do you know when to stop the business of life and Be Present the being in life?

Lesson: Identify ways in which you're being present and prioritizing your relationship. Choose one area you would like to enhance, and take action to improve that area.

2. Do and Be Your Best

Setting the intention to Do and Be Your Best is a helpful tool that creates a mind-set that sets you up for success and happiness.

Even though Do and Be Your Best might be part of your core values for life in general, it is important to evaluate and explore how you practice this in your Mindful Loving relationship. Your Mindful Loving relationship presents the stage for you to act out your best and worst parts. It is a daily challenge to do and be your best.

Mindful Loving allows you and your partner to notice and challenge each other to Do and Be Your Best. Your partner holds the mirror to reflect back to you whether or not you are attuned to the practice of doing and being your best.

The practice of doing and being your best is simple, and not always easy. Doing and being your best starts with intention which is followed by action. The intention is to Do and Be Your Best, and the practice is to put that intention into action.

Exercise for Do and Be Your Best

Be mindful throughout the day, and check in to ensure that you are being and acting your best.

Some questions to ask yourself include the following:

- In what ways did I do my best?
- How well did I love, care for, and nurture myself and my partner?
- How well did I keep my promises to myself and to others?
- How was I part of the solution instead of part of the problem?
- How well did I use the Practical Tools for Mindful Loving?

Lesson: Commit to do and be your best as individuals. This practice will flow into your Mindful Loving relationship and enhance the passion and purpose of Mindful Lovin

3. Use "I" Messages

The use of "I" Messages is one of the most important and powerful practices used in Mindful Loving relationships. This skill simply involves owning and talking about your own experience. It involves saying what you are thinking, feeling, and wanting. Using "I" Messages is easier when you speak from a place of honesty and openness about your own experience.

For example:

> "I am so frustrated that you didn't pick up the dry cleaning. I needed to have one of those dresses to wear to work tomorrow."

Even when you are frustrated with your partner's behavior, it is important to stay focused on your own experience.

Be careful about camouflaged "I" Messages that are really "You" Messages. "You" Messages usually include judgments and complaints.

Consider the following example:

> "I am frustrated that you are so irresponsible and forgot to pick up the dry cleaning! Now I must find something else to wear to work tomorrow. I feel like you don't even care about me or my needs."

See the difference? The "You" Message makes a judgment: "You are so irresponsible." It also involves a complaint or an assumption: "I feel like you don't even care about me or my needs. This "You" Message is more about your partner and not focused on your own experience.

Using "You" Messages leads to unloving and unhealthy communication, filled with judgments, criticism, and assumptions. Judgments and assumptions are destructive forms of communication and lead to hurt, anger and emotional distance

Also, be careful about using the phrases "feel like" and "feel that" when you are using "I" Messages.

Consider the following example:

"I feel like you never listen to me."

When you use the phrase, "I feel like" or "I feel that," you are stating a belief, not a feeling. It is more accurate and honest to say the following:

"I feel upset when I think you are not listening."

When you use words that describe your emotions e.g., "I feel sad," "I feel mad," or "I feel happy", you are sharing an honest and real feeling that leads to greater intimacy.

Lesson: Practice using, "I" Messages to enhance the effectiveness of Loving Communication.

4. Listen from the Heart to Understand

Listen from the Heart to Understand is a necessary and important practice for building emotional intimacy. It is about listening to understand what your partner is saying and feeling. It is driven by a sincere desire to know and understand what your partner is trying to tell you. One of the most loving things you can do for your partner is to listen and understand.

To Listen from the Heart to Understand, you must put your own opinions, judgments, and responses on hold. It is impossible to listen and really hear your partner while you are busy constructing your response to what is being said. Listening to understand what your partner is saying and feeling requires that you give your full attention without distractions or interruptions.

Exercise for Listen from the Heart to Understand

- Your partner starts a conversation:

    "I have something I would like to talk about. Is this a good time?"

- You respond with the following:

    "Yes." (or set another specific time for the conversation.)

- Take a deep breath, and set your intention to listen. Listen attentively to hear and capture all the details of the communication.

- When your partner has finished, respond with a confirmation of what you heard:

    "So, what I hear is that you were upset and worried when I didn't call. Is that right?"

- Check with your partner to see if you got it right, and then pause to wait for your partner's response.

- Wait for your partner to say something like the following:

    "Yes, you got it. Thanks."

- You can then continue with the conversation.

    If you did not get it right, go back and ask for clarification. It might be helpful to say, "Tell me more," or "Help me understand what you are saying."

The key to Listen from the Heart to Understand is to listen, not to speak.

It is very difficult to Listen from the Heart to Understand when your partner is saying something negative about you. When you hear a negative comment about yourself, a natural response is to defend or explain yourself. It takes practice to stop the habit of a defensive response and use this tool.

Even when your partner uses old communication patterns of judgments, criticism, and assumptions, you can practice the skill, Listen from the Heart to Understand and break the old patterns of miscommunication.

The benefit of this tool is learning to listen carefully to really understand what your partner is saying and how your partner is feeling. The experience of being heard and understood is profound and fulfills a significant purpose in Mindful Loving.

Lesson: Practice Listen from the Heart to Understand.

5. Practice Balanced Communication

It is important to have a balance in our communication. If one partner does all the talking, or one partner doesn't talk much at all, the quality of the communication will suffer. Loving Communication involves a balance in which both partners speak and both partners listen.

The tool, Practice Balanced Communication, makes you more mindful and intentional about your Loving Communication. Both partners trying to talk and listen at the same time is a common problem. All too often, as you are listening to your partner, you are constructing your own response to what is being said. This habit causes you to disengage from your partner and focus on your own response instead of what your partner is saying.

In the practice of Balanced Communication, one person speaks and one person listens; then they reverse roles.

Exercise for Balanced Communication

- Ask your partner for five minutes to practice this tool.

- One partner agrees to speak first, and the other partner agrees to listen first.

- One partner starts expressing a desire to discuss a particular concern:

  "I am really stressed about work and would like to talk to you about it."

- The other partner agrees to listen or negotiates a time for full attention.

- The first partner continues expressing his or her concern:

  "I am so frustrated with my new manager. He is changing my responsibilities, and I don't know how long I will have this job."

- The other partner listens and shares what he or she has heard.

    "So, what I hear you saying is that your manager is changing your responsibilities, and you are worried you are going to get fired. Is that right?"

- The first partner appreciates and agrees that the other partner's assessment is accurate.

    "Yes, I am really scared I might lose this job. I don't know what this manager is up to."

- The other partner then responds as follows:

    "Thank you for sharing this. This must be hard for you. Is there anything I can do to help?"

- The first partner thanks the partner for listening and being supportive.

- They then reverse roles, continuing to Practice Balanced Communication.

Communication Balance is really a serial monologue in which one person speaks while the other person listens. The tool, Practice Balanced Communication, allows one partner to feel heard, understood, and validated by the other partner. When this happens, you feel an emotional connection, and it becomes easier to switch roles and listen to your partner.

Lesson: Practice Balanced Communication regularly so it becomes second nature to you.

6. Be Mindful of Your Thoughts

Don't believe everything you think. Some thoughts are not necessarily the truth. Just because a thought enters your mind does not mean you should believe it. You can change any thought to create a more mindful and loving thought.

Mindful questions to ask yourself to evaluate a thought include the following:

> "Is this thought really true?"
> "Is this thought helping me or hurting me?"
> "How is this thought impacting my feelings about myself or my partner?"

In your relationship with yourself, you might think negative thoughts, such as

> *I feel fat and ugly. I can't believe you find me sexy or attractive.*

In evaluating this thought, you might discover that you really believe it to be true, which causes you to hide or avoid sexual contact.

A more honest and vulnerable thought would be

> *Even though I am uncomfortable, it is time for me to learn to love and take care of my body.*

In your relationship with your partner, you can think critical thoughts, such as

> *You don't care how I feel, when you are always late.*

In evaluating this thought, you might find that it is not true and that it hurts you and makes you feel angry at your partner.

A more mindful and loving thought would be

> *I know you care about me. Your being late is a problem for you and does not reflect about how you feel about me. I want to talk more about this and how we can resolve this problem.*

Just because a thought enters your mind does not mean you need to say it aloud. Once you have evaluated the truth of your thought, you then can decide whether or not to share it.

Mindful questions to ask yourself about sharing your thoughts are as follows:

> "Have I accepted responsibility for my thoughts?"
> "Would sharing these thoughts be helpful?"

When you decide to share a thought, it is important to use "I" Messages.

Lesson: Be Mindful of Your Thoughts. Thoughts become your beliefs.

7. Be Mindful of Your Emotions

There are three steps that will help you Be Mindful of Your Emotions.

1. Recognize the emotion.
2. Reflect on the emotion.
3. Respond to the emotional experience.

1. Recognize the Emotion

Emotions are a natural part of being human. Emotions are an instinctive and authentic part of who you are. Basic emotions include joy, surprise, sadness, fear, anger, and disgust. There are many different feelings attached to these basic emotions.

When you experience fear, you might feel uneasy, anxious, or terrified. These emotional responses are part of your survival system. When you experience joy, you might feel happy, loving, or ecstatic. These emotions help you feel connected to others. When you experience surprise, you might feel delight, shock, or insecurity. Your emotional experiences and responses help you understand yourself, others, and the world around you.

Practices that can help you recognize your emotions include the following:

1. Be aware and honest about what emotion you are feeling.
2. Ask yourself, "Am I feeling hurt (or jealous, angry, excited, loved, etc.)?"
3. Identify and name the emotion. When you name it, you can tame it.

2. Reflect on the Emotion

You have thoughts, judgments, and stories about your emotional experiences. These thoughts, judgments, and stories contribute to your emotional experiences and responses. When you recognize and respect your thoughts about the emotional experience, you can more mindfully respond to a wide range of situations.

84

Practices to help you reflect on your emotions include the following:

1. Be aware of the thoughts, judgments, and stories attached to the emotional experience, and if they are not helpful, change them.

    "I am so hurt that you forgot our anniversary. I don't believe you love me like you used to."

2. Ask yourself, "How are these thoughts, judgments, or stories helpful or hurtful to me?"

    "The thought that you don't love me like you used to makes me feel hurt and sad and I know that this is not true."

3. Think about ways you can change negative or hurtful thoughts, judgments, or stories.

    "When you remember things that are important to me, I feel loved by you. Although you were preoccupied by work and forgot the day of our anniversary, the plans you made to celebrate on the weekend tell me that you really do love me."

3. Respond to the Emotional Experience

Responding is a mindful practice that enables you to be more intentional, thoughtful, and loving. Emotions have energy, and it is important to find outlets to express, evaluate, and direct that energy.

Practices to help you respond to your emotional experience include the following:

1. Respond. Don't react!

    Reacting is something you do automatically, without thinking. A reaction is an action that does not engage the mind and can feel mindless rather than mindful. Reacting to an emotion can involve a physical reaction in your body and can lead you to say or do something that might be hurtful, and that you may later regret. Feeling angry doesn't necessarily mean you must react with yelling or saying mean things. Feeling scared doesn't mean you react by running away or shutting your partner out.

2. Find a healthy release for the intensity for the emotional experience. For example, do one of the following:

   - Go for a walk.
   - Meditate or pray.
   - Talk to someone.
   - Journal.
   - Breathe.

3. Evaluate the emotional experience. Ask yourself the following questions:

   "Are these feelings triggered by old negative experiences and thoughts?"

   "Right now, what else is going on with me that contributes to my reaction? Am I tired, hungry, sick, or feeling disconnected?"

   "What do I want, and how do I express it respectfully?"

4. Make an intentional choice about how to respond to the situation. You might

   - Resolve the emotional experience internally without taking further action;
   - Reflect about ways to respond and then speak up or take an action; or
   - Respond with honesty, respect, and clarity.

Lesson: Stop, think, and be intentional with your responses.

8. Puke Recycled Emotions

Recycled emotions are emotions that cause you to feel unhealthy and continue to creep into your life and grab you with an intensity that disables your mindful practices.

When you continue to eat something that has made you sick in the past, your body will eliminate it by vomiting. Similarly, there are times when you have unhealthy repetitive thoughts and feelings that also make you sick. These negative and toxic thoughts and feelings need to be eliminated as well. When you ignore these intense thoughts and feelings, they end up making you feel worse, just as you end up feeling worse when you try to avoid throwing up. One of the ways to eliminate those negative and toxic thoughts and feelings is by puking recycled emotions

Physical Puking

When you need to physically throw up, you don't

- ignore it,
- allow yourself to puke all over others,
- hold on to or analyze the contents of the vomit, or
- give value to toxic or undigested food.

Instead, you recognize the need to vomit, provide a space to puke, and flush the contents down the toilet. As unpleasant as puking can be, it allows your body to rid itself of unhealthy elements in order to feel better.

Just as there are times when you need to physically throw up, there are also times when you need to emotionally puke.

Emotional Puking

There are times when you need to emotionally puke unhealthy and recycled emotions. These are times when you should not

- ignore the intensity of your emotions,

- spew angry or toxic words at your partner,
- hold on to the emotional charge of the story, or
- give value to the content by defending the emotional puke.

Remember, there are no benefits to holding on to the contents of emotional vomit!

Instead, you recognize the need to release and purge your unhealthy and recycled thoughts and feelings. You find a safe time and place to emotionally puke recycled and unhealthy emotions to release the emotional toxicity and resolve the emotional distress.

Basic Guidelines for Puking Recycled Emotions with Your Partner:

1. Recognize that you need to emotionally puke. Take responsibility for the content of the story behind your emotional distress.

2. Let your partner know that you need to emotionally puke so you can clear the air.

3. Find a safe and private place. It is not mindful to puke in front of your children or friends or in public.

4. Talk about what is upsetting you without being critical or hurtful. Be concise and specific.

5. Your partner should mindfully stand by while you puke without analyzing or holding on to the story even if it involves him or her.

6. Let your partner know when you are finished puking and share the root of the emotional distress.

7. Let your partner know what, if anything, you need to help you feel better.

Consider the following example of Emotional Puking:

1. Megan recognizes she is feeling hurt and angry.
2. She tells Michael she needs to puke. He agrees and prepares to listen and be there for her.
3. They agree to talk in their bedroom.
4. She begins to yell and cry about how overwhelmed she feels and how frustrated she is that he doesn't help her around the house. Michael follows the guidelines and listens. He tells himself that Meagan is really upset, and he needs only to let her puke her feelings. He reminds himself that he loves her, and this is about her feelings, not about him.
5. After about ten minutes, she takes a deep breath and says she's finished puking. She recognizes that the root of her distress is that she overcommits, doesn't practice enough self-care, and does not get the help she needs from him.
6. Megan thanks Michael for listening and asks him to help her recognize times when she is overcommitting.
7. They agree to make time to reevaluate their schedules and chores.

Lesson: Practice Emotional Puking Recycled Emotions on less intense issues first. As with any other tool, the more you practice it, the easier and more skilled you will become at it.

9. Use The 5 To 1 Appreciation Rule

Give 5 words of appreciation for each criticism or complaint. Words of appreciation enhance your ability to deal with challenges and difficulties in your relationship. Words of appreciation help you and your partner feel important and validated. Appreciation boosts your spirits and raises self-confidence. We all need to feel valued for who we are and for our accomplishments and our contributions.

Criticism is destructive and tears us down. It is a communication practice that results in hurt, denigration, or harm. Chronic criticism is abusive, erodes the core of love, and decreases passion in a relationship. Criticism is a common practice that many have learned and used, and it is important to eliminate criticism from your communication practices. It is normal to have complaints; however, it is never okay to inflict criticism on yourself or your partner. It is an important practice to recognize complaints and express them respectfully with each other.

The 5 To 1 Ratio Rule lays the foundation for trust and respect. This tool means you give 5 words of appreciation for every criticism or complaint. The use of this tool enables you to address the normal challenges, complaints, and difficulties more effectively.

It is equally important to monitor your own self-talk and treat yourself with the same practice of appreciation and respect you use with your partner. You can redirect yourself and use the Basics of Mindful Loving-Loving Communication and Understanding & Respecting Differences - to find a resolution to your challenges.

Exercise for the 5 To 1 Ratio Rule

- Make an agreement to use the 5 To 1 Ratio Rule.

- Start with one day at a time.

- Follow the rule, and evaluate your own progress with your own self-talk as well as the communication with your partner.

Lesson: Use the 5 To 1 Ratio Rule and practice it daily.

10. Have Daily Big Talk Conversations

Big Talk conversations is a time to talk with each other about what is important to you. It allows you to create moments of intimacy and connection through talking about what you are feeling and thinking. You share the joys and accomplishments as well as the challenges and disappointments. Spending this quality time is essential for Mindful Loving. Big Talk conversations is necessary to maintain emotional connection and helps you build and enrich your passion.

Living together and loving each other doesn't necessarily provide a regular opportunity for meaningful conversations, or Big Talk conversations. Life gets so busy with work, kids, school, and the stuff of daily living that you often don't make time to really connect. When you don't use the tool, Have Daily Big Talk Conversations, you end up only having small talk conversations. Small talk is about what is going on around you or with others.

It is necessary that both partners agree on the importance of Big Talk. The best way to have Big Talk is to set time aside that allows for uninterrupted conversation. There are some days when Big Talk conversations might only be a brief connection and might take more time. Some partners find their best time for daily Big Talk conversation is before they go to bed. Others schedule it for after dinner. It does not matter how or when you do it; the most important thing is to have Big Talk conversations.

Some examples of daily Big Talk conversation include how you think and feel about the following:

- daily life experiences
- celebrations and accomplishments
- hurt, angry, sad, or scared feelings
- requests for love and support
- your sexual relationship
- communication and miscommunication
- family challenges

- finances
- family and friends
- social commitments
- work commitments
- recreation and relaxation time

The essence of this tool is that you prioritize time for intimacy and connection.

Lesson: Use the term Big Talk as a cue to invite your partner into conversation and connection.

11. Have Small Talk and Share Your Day

Small Talk involves sharing stories and experiences about what is going on around you. You and your partner each have different experiences throughout your day. Small Talk helps you fill in the gaps you might have missed with each other during your day. Small Talk is the bridge to Big Talk because it helps you stay current and connected with each other.

Some examples of Small Talk and Share Your Day includes stories about the following:

- things that happened at work
- things that happened with the kids
- a conversation you had with another person
- the mundane, meaningful, or funny experiences you had during the day
- news or current events

The use of this tool preserves our connection and nurtures our Mindful Loving experience with each other.

Lesson: Make time every day to share your day with each other.

12. Maintain Contact When You Talk

There are three points of contact important to use when you are talking with each other. The three points of contact are as follows:

- Be in the same room.
- Maintain eye contact.
- Touch.

Although it might seem obvious, it is critical to be in the same room when you talk with each other. How often have you found yourself talking to your partner from another room or responding as you are walking away?

Be proactive. If you realize you and your partner are talking from different rooms, stop the conversation and move into a shared space. It only takes one of you to make that move.

Maintaining eye contact when you talk with each other shows that you are giving your full attention. Eye contact reflects your openness and willingness to engage. When you maintain eye contact during a conversation, you are not checking your phone, looking at the TV, or working on your computer. Maintaining eye contact results in feeling connected and important. This tool reinforces prioritizing each other and enhances empathy and understanding.

When you are talking, a gentle touch of your partner's hand, arm or shoulder increases your connection. This kind of touch triggers the release of oxytocin, the bonding hormone, and promotes a feeling of safety and connection. In our tech-dominated society, you can often feel touch deprived. This tool helps you feel good and can soothe and heal. Make sure you refrain from touch in violent exchanges or if you don't feel safe.

Lesson: Make a conscious decision to be in the same room, maintain eye contact, and touch each other when you talk.

13. Make Time for Affection

Affection is the gentle feeling of fondness and caring for your partner. It is the tender attachment you feel as a result of your Mindful Loving. The experience and the expression of affection vary from person to person. You each must identify your own preferences for affection.

Some partners are more comfortable with physical expressions and tend to give that to their partners and want it in return. These partners enjoy things like cuddling, holding hands, and hugging. Others might be more verbal

in expressing affection. They enjoy sharing tender words, compliments, and appreciations and saying, "I love you." Still, other partners express and experience affection by doing acts of love and kindness. These partners might do things like bring flowers or gifts, wash their partners' cars, or bring their partners a favorite cup of coffee or tea.

By practicing the Golden Rule of Mindful Loving, which involves loving your partner the way your partner wants to be loved, you identify your own preferences and your partner's preferences for affection. This helps you Make Time for Affection that is mutually meaningful.

To Make Time for Affection consider the following practices:

- Be mindful, and hug each other four or more times a day. Common times are after waking up, when leaving the house, when returning from the day, and before going to bed at night.
- Take a moment in the morning or evening to spoon or snuggle.
- Touch each other during the day: hold hands, touch your partner's knee in the car or under the table, or stop doing the dishes or brushing your teeth to lean into your partner's hug.
- Use Big Talk conversations to share words of affection when you are talking about your day with each other.
- Write love notes and leave them on your partner's pillow or in the car. Send love texts during the day or when you are sitting on the couch next to each other.

95

- Give a single flower, favorite treat, or gift to your partner.
- Perform simple acts of kindness, such as doing the dishes, running an errand, or making the bed.
- Take care of the children to allow for your partner's self-care time.

Lesson: Practice making time for affection daily.

14. Create a Mindful Loving Gratitude Journal

Creating a Mindful Loving Gratitude Journal is a tool that helps you focus on what you feel grateful for and what you appreciate about your partner. A Mindful Loving Gratitude Journal is one of the best ways to prioritize and emotionally nurture your relationship.

Gratitude is food for your soul. Acknowledging and expressing gratitude and appreciation activates the law of attraction - what you give attention to multiplies. What you appreciate in life you get more of.

It is not always easy to balance everything and maintain a high level of nurturing and care in your relationship. Mindful Loving helps you set the intention of prioritizing your relationship.

The guidelines for using a Mindful Loving Gratitude Journal are simple:

1. First, talk to your partner about a Mindful Loving Gratitude Journal, and ask him or her to join you in using the tool.
2. Get a spiral notebook, and tie a pen to the notebook so you will be ready to write in your journal and always have the pen available.
3. Put the notebook in the bathroom next to the toilet. Yes, next to the toilet! It's a place you spend some alone time every day. It's the perfect place to take a few minutes to use this tool and write in the Mindful Loving Gratitude Journal.
4. Every day, while you are on the toilet, pick up the notebook and write one or more things that you appreciate or feel grateful for about your partner. Be specific and creative, and keep it simple and personal.

Consider the following examples:

"I am so grateful that you are in my life."
"I appreciate that you made the bed this morning."
"I really appreciate that you listened to me while I was complaining about my boss."
"I really enjoyed our wild and wonderful lovemaking last night."

5. Each day, read your partner's journal entry and then make your own entry.

There are variations for using a Mindful Loving Gratitude Journal:

- Write in a notebook that you keep in another designated location.
- Text or email each other. This works well when one partner is out of town or not available to write in the notebook.

Make a commitment to write every day. Don't judge or criticize yourself or your partner if you miss a day or two. If your partner gets off track, keep your own writing on track. It is important to remember that writing what you appreciate about your partner is also a gift you give yourself. Your commitment to the practice of keeping an attitude of gratitude positively affects your day, your relationship, and your life.

An additional benefit of using the Mindful Loving Gratitude Journal is being able to reread it on days when you are feeling sad, hurt, frustrated, or angry. Flooding your brain with the journal entries of appreciation and statements of gratitude shifts the neurochemistry in the brain and generates a sense of well-being and connection. This practice puts you in a better mood! Focusing on what you appreciate in your relationship helps those things grow and multiply.

Imagine the rich and loving journal you will be creating to capture the best of your Mindful Loving relationship. This simple tool is one of the best and easiest ways to stay connected and emotionally nurture your relationship.

Lesson: Create a Mindful Loving Gratitude Journal and use it every day.

15. Practice Acts of Kindness

Acts of Kindness are expressions of love and care that send messages like the following:

> "I love you."
> "I am thinking about you and want to brighten your day."
> "You are important and special to me."

When couples Practice Acts of Kindness from a place of unconditional love with no expectation of receiving anything in return, these acts have a positive effect on both partners. Acts of kindness strengthen your immune system and increases neurochemicals that make you feel good.

The effects of acts of kindness are turbocharged when these acts of kindness are in alignment with what your partner defines as meaningful.

Examples of Practice Acts of Kindness include the following:

- placing a piece of chocolate on a pillow
- leaving a love note on the windshield
- making your partner's favorite meal
- purchasing a special coffee or treat
- doing your partner's chore
- sending a suggestive love text
- acknowledging your partner's accomplishment
- gifting tickets to your partner's favorite event

The tool, Practice Acts of Kindness is a powerful gesture of love. The use of this tool gives you and your partner simple opportunities to feel good, spread kindness, and enhance Mindful Loving.

Lesson: Be creative and create your own lists of acts of kindness. Practice daily, and share your list with your partner.

16. Lighten Up and Laugh Together (LULT)

Stop, take a deep breath, and lighten up! Sometimes, you need to take a break and lighten up because you can become too serious. To lighten up is a choice you make that allows you to expand your perceptions. Every day you get the opportunity to broaden your perspective. You can choose to view any situation from the perspective of the glass being half full or half empty. The perception of half full is a choice you make to view the positive side of any situation. This ability develops as a result of your commitment to self-care and self-love. The perception of half empty is a choice you make that limits you.

Laughing is one of the best things you can do for yourself. Laughter is contagious, and it lifts your spirits and helps you feel good in the moment. Laughter is an effective way to decrease stress and release endorphins that decrease pain and enhance your health.

Lighten Up and Laugh Together is a tool that helps you and your partner maintain your sense of connection and intimacy. Finding humor and laughing together floods your relationship with positive emotions.

Do you remember a time when you heard something funny and couldn't wait to share it with your partner? Sharing laughter together strengthens the choice of seeing life situations as half full. Those moments bring more joy and nurture your connection with each other.

Some ways to Lighten Up and Laugh Together include the following:

- Watch a comedy.
- Listen to music that makes you want to dance.
- Share funny stories.
- Watch videos of babies laughing or animals doing silly things.

Lesson: Every day set the intention to LULT: Lighten Up and Laugh Together.

17. Play Together

Play helps you have fun and interact with the world around you. Play allows you to be creative, passionate, and imaginative. Sometimes as adults we forget how to play. Play is a wonderful way to keep the fun and joy flowing in your Mindful Loving relationship.

Some examples of using this tool include the following:

- Build fun into mundane things, such as grocery shopping, cleaning the house, running errands, or exercising together.
- Plan play dates to go hiking or go to the park or playground.
- Text your partner and invite him or her to do something fun together.
- Leave flirtatious, silly, or love notes on each other's pillow, desk, or car.
- Play games together, laugh, and let yourselves be silly.
- Take a class together, such as painting, ceramics, cooking, acting, gardening, or nutrition classes.

Lesson: Keep play, passion, and connection alive in your relationship every day.

18. Maintain Connection through Writing

Writing is a useful tool to maintain emotional connection. Writing enables you to reflect and gain clarity with what you are thinking and feeling.

Guidelines to start writing include the following:

- Create your own list of easy and fun reflective topics. Here are some examples:

  What is the best date, vacation, or event we have shared together?

  What do I love most about you?

  What is a memory of us that makes me laugh?

  What is the most romantic time we have had together?
- Make an agreement that each of you will write for five minutes on a topic.
- Write for five minutes without editing.
- Each partner should then read his or her writing aloud while the other listens with an open heart.

There are times in Mindful Loving when you might feel hurt and disconnected. This tool will help you first gain clarity about what you are experiencing and then enable you to communicate and reconnect with your partner.

Guidelines for reflective writing when you feel hurt or disconnected are as follows:

- Take five minutes to write about the hurt. Some examples include the following:

  "I feel disconnected because..."

  "I feel most hurt about..."

  "I miss the way we used to..."

  "What I would like to change is..."
- Ask your partner to listen while you share your writing.
- Your partner should Listen from the Heart to Understand.

This practice will help you have Big Talk conversations. Using this tool helps you be honest with yourself and maintain emotional connection with your partner. You get to practice the Basics of Mindful Loving through the use of Loving Communication with yourself and your partner, which results in Understanding & Respecting Differences.

Lesson: Create your own list of reflective topics and expand it as your relationship grows.

19. Schedule Regular Dates with Each Other

Regular dates are important for maintaining the passion and purpose in your Mindful Loving relationship. Passion ignites mental, emotional, physical, sexual, and spiritual intimacy. Scheduling regular dates is a way to prioritize each other and the relationship. Regular dates fulfill the purpose of having stimulating conversation, emotional connection, physical touch and affection, sexual and sensual play, and spiritual interconnection.

A Mindful Loving date is defined as follows:

D – Direct
A – Attention
T – Toward
E – Each Other

It gives you the opportunity to use the following tools:

Have Small Talk and Share Your Day
Lighten Up and Laugh Together
Play Together
Maintain Connection through Writing

When regular dates are not scheduled, they don't happen. Regular dates are opportunities to stop and focus on each other, not on children, work, or family.

Some examples of dates include the following:

- Have a picnic at home.
- Watch a sunset or sunrise.
- Dance in your living room.
- Go to a new restaurant or coffee shop.
- Attend a local performing arts event.
- Go on a hike.

Be creative in scheduling regular dates. Dates can happen in the morning, the middle of the day, or the evening. They can take place at home as well as away from home and don't have to cost a lot of money.

Engaging in regular dates without the expectation that a date will automatically end in sexual connection allows you to mindfully focus on being present and enjoy each other.

Scheduling regular dates creates the foundation that ignites and maintains your passion, purpose, and connection with each other.

Lesson: Be creative and have fun scheduling regular dates.

20. Schedule Sensual and Sexual Dates

It is estimated that 15 percent to 20 percent of North American couples live in a sexless marriage. Many couples don't prioritize and invest time and energy in keeping their romantic and sexual relationship active and alive.

Couples take time to plan for many things and events in their lives. They plan for their financial future, vacations, holidays, and social gatherings It is also important to schedule time for romance and sexual connection. Without scheduling the time, it's easy to let other things get in the way and risk not making time for these important connections.

Schedule Time for Sensual and Sexual Dates means you both agree to prioritize time and energy to invest in connecting with each other. Sensual and sexual dates provide the opportunity to reignite the passion, purpose, and romance experienced earlier in the relationship.

Sexual dates are not just about having sex. There is much more to sexual intimacy and connection. The foundation of sexual intimacy starts with sensual pleasuring. Sensual pleasuring focuses on the five senses: sight, smell, taste, sound, and touch. Using your five senses helps you awaken desire and enhance pleasure.

When thinking about sensual pleasuring, ask yourself the following:

- What do I see that brings pleasure? Perhaps I see the lighting in the room, the soft flicker of a candle, the look in my partner's eyes or the contour of our bodies.
- What are some of the smells that are pleasurable? Perhaps I smell the fragrance of flowers, perfumes, essential oils, or the natural erotic aroma of my partner's body.
- What are some of the tastes that please me? Perhaps I taste foods such as chocolate, strawberries, or wine, or the taste of my partner's kisses.

- What sounds do I enjoy? Perhaps I hear music in the background or the sound of my partner's voice sharing words of love and affirmation.
- What touch feels pleasurable? Perhaps I feel of my partner's skin and hair, the feel of fresh sheets on my body, or my partner's gentle, sensual massage.

Answer these questions for yourself, and then share them with your partner. Listen to your responses to these questions and create a fun plan for sensual pleasuring in your Mindful Loving relationship.

Sexual dates focus on physical, sensual, and sexual desire and pleasure. They're about connecting and having fun together. Some couples are turned off by the idea of scheduling a sexual date because it sounds unromantic. Many believe that, sex should happen spontaneously and easily. However, when you schedule time for romantic and sexual dates, there is an opportunity for natural spontaneity. Spontaneity is more about the experience of what happens during your sexual date than the expectation of the sexual date spontaneously occurring.

Some ideas for sexual dates include the following:

- Take turns initiating and planning a sexual date.
- Give each other sensual massages or take baths or showers together.
- Share sexual fantasies with each other.
- Read about ideas that can help spice up your sexual relationship.
- Make lists of your sexual wants, and share them with each other.
- Plan time to kiss, hug, neck, and have fun with no expectation of intercourse.

Schedule Time for Sensual and Sexual Dates. It provides a positive expectation and is a sign that you are prioritizing and nurturing your relationship. It strengthens and adds zest to your Mindful Loving relationship.

Lesson: Mix it up and have fun planning your sensual and sexual dates.

21. Create Your Own Sensual and Sexual Menu

There is no good common language for talking about sex. Sexual talk usually means either resorting to clinical terms such as coitus, penis, and vagina, or using more common street terms. Most couples don't feel comfortable with either format and struggle with talking about their sexual relationship.

This tool, Create Your Own Sensual and Sexual Menu is a fun tool that helps couples start the conversation about their sexual relationship. There are many parallels between our appetites for sex and our appetites for food. Just as a menu in a restaurant describes food choices and their contents, a sensual and sexual menu offers a format for creating your own unique sensual and sexual experience with each other.

The Sexual Menu gives each of you an opportunity to describe and define your sensual and sexual desires, pleasures, and experiences. It is a simple activity that gives you and your partner your own sexual language to talk about your own unique sexual appetites and sexual practices.

How to Create a Your Own Sensual and Sexual Menu:

1. First, think about a menu from a restaurant. Choose a meal from a restaurant menu. It can be a breakfast, lunch, dinner, or dessert item. For breakfast, you might choose eggs benedict or a smoothie.

2. Now think about a sexual experience you've had that would be your eggs benedict, an early morning gourmet sexual experience. For example, you might describe this using a memory of a leisurely sexual experience you had during a vacation - a time when you both had time to relax and enjoy a prolonged, delicious lovemaking experience. Think about a sexual experience that would be your smoothie, an early morning quickie sexual experience in which both partners start the day with a quick and rich sexual and intimate connection.

3. Describe the details of your sexual experience. This helps you create your own sexual language. Developing your own sensual

and sexual menu helps you know and communicate the sexual experiences you want in your Mindful Loving relationship.

4. Write down as many items as you like to describe your breakfast, lunch, dinner, and dessert sexual experiences. They can range from quickies to gourmet lovemaking sessions.

Consider some of the following examples of sensual and sexual menus:

Sensual and Sexual Breakfast Menu

Eggs Benedict: Gourmet, delicious early lovemaking with time for both to orgasm

Smoothie: An early morning quickie

Sensual and Sexual Lunch Menu

Hamburger: A familiar love making session squeezed into the middle of the day

Salad: A light, easy time of playing together sensually and sexually

Sensual and Sexual Dinner Menu

Grilled salmon: Gourmet lovemaking with lots of time for erotic touch, tenderness, and play culminating in mutually pleasurable orgasms.

Pizza: Turning to each other, kissing, and having intercourse before going to sleep

Sensual and Sexual Dessert Menu

Cheesecake: Basking in enjoying in the afterglow after sex and holding each other

Fruit and cheese: Cuddling and kissing on the couch together.

The most important part of the Create Your Own Sensual and Sexual Menu tool is developing and sharing the tool to fit your sexual appetites, desires, and pleasures. It gives you a common language, a shortcut to describe your sexual appetites, and a shared understanding of what you each want for your sexual intimacy and experiences.

Lesson: Create Your Own Sensual and Sexual Menu. Use your imagination and have fun!

22. Ignite and Maintain Romance

Romance in your Mindful Loving relationship maintains the connection, passion, mystery, and excitement of being with each other. Romance creates a reserve that enables you to cope with challenges that come up in life together.

Each partner has his or her own unique expectation and experience with romance. Some partners experience romance when they receive gifts or are showered with love and compliments, and for others, romance is ignited when there is an experience that involves erotic sexual play and lovemaking; a thoughtful dinner; or flirtatious gestures that say, "I want you. You are my special person."

Some ideas to help Ignite and Maintain Romance include the following:

- Share ideas about what romance is for each of you.
- Talk about past activities that you thought were romantic.
- Agree to make plans to infuse romance into your everyday life.
- Take turns planning fun and romantic experiences.
- Use books, podcasts, or apps to help you come up with ideas for romance.
- Practice "choreplay"-surprising your partner by doing his or her chore.

Lesson: Talk about your romantic expectations and desires with each other.

23. Practice Center-Stage Communication

Center-Stage communication is a highly effective tool to use for Big Talk and or tough talks. These are conversations when you or your partner is hurt, angry, or worried. This tool helps you stay on track when the conversation is emotionally charged. It helps you create a safe place to talk about difficult issues.

Center-Stage Communication is a ten-step practice based upon an agreement that one person talks while the other person listens. It is important for person A to be clear and use "I" Messages. Similarly, it is important for person B to be present and Listen from the Heart to Understand. This tool might seem overwhelming at first. With practice it begins to flow more naturally.

The partner who asks for Center-Stage Communication is person A the other partner is person B.

Step 1   Person A recognizes he or she has an issue or problem.
- Identify the problem or issue. (Keep it simple—only one issue at a time.)
- Rate it on a scale of importance and intensity from 1 to 5, with 1 being minimal, 3 being moderate, and 5 being maximum distress,

Example: Hank recognizes he is upset with Sonya for the amount of time she spends on her phone.
- He is upset about her being on the phone when they spend time together.
- He rates his level of distress as a 4.

Step 2   Person A invites person B for Center-Stage Communication.
- Ask for Center-Stage Communication time: "I want to talk to you using Center-Stage Communication. Is this a good time for you? If not, when is?"
- Set a time limit for how long it will take: "It will take fifteen minutes of your undivided attention."

Example: Hank asks Sonya for Center-Stage Communication.

- Hank says, "I want to talk to you using Center-Stage Communication. Is this a good time for you?"
- "I would like fifteen minutes of your undivided attention."

Step 3 Person B agrees to Center-Stage Communication and agrees to listen.

- Take responsibility to be present and Listen from the Heart to Understand person A.
- Person B is committed to listen and understand person A's experience of the issue or problem.
- Person B listens without defending or explaining.

Example: Sonya agrees to Center-Stage Communication and agrees to listen.

- Sonya takes responsibility to be present and listen to Hank from her heart.
- As much as she might want to defend herself, Sonya is committed to listen and understand Hank's experience.

Step 4 Person A shares the problem or issue.

- Take responsibility, and use "I" Messages to communicate the issue or problem.
- Upon completion, tell person B, "Please tell me what you heard me say so I know you got it."

Example: Hank shares his upset about her being on the phone when he is with her.

- Hank says, "I am really frustrated. We don't have a lot of alone time together, and it seems that whenever we are together, you are on the phone. I feel not important and disconnected from you. It is as if I have to compete for your attention."

- Hank closes with, "Please tell me what you heard me say so I know you got it."

Step 5 Person B summarizes what he or she heard.
- Respond with what was heard: "Let me try to summarize what I heard you say. (Paraphrase the issue.) Did I hear you correctly?"
- Person B only responds to what was said without adding opinions, judgments, or explanations.

Example: Sonya responds with what she heard.
Sonya resists her desire to defend herself. She focuses on Hank and says, "What I heard you say is you don't like that I am on my phone so much." "Is that correct?"

Step 6 Person A confirms or clarifies what person B said.
- If person A believes person B heard correctly, say, "Yes. Thank you for listening to me."
- If person A does not believe person B heard correctly, say,
  "Let's try this again to clarify what I want you to know."
- Repeat steps 4 and 5 as many times as necessary until person A feels heard and understood.

Example: Hank clarifies what he said.
- Hank says, "Let's try this again. What I am really upset about is the amount of time you are on your phone when we are just hanging out together in the car, at dinner, or watching TV."
- Sonya repeats step 5 and says, "So what you are upset about is that I am on my phone when we are hanging out together, because it makes you feel unimportant. Is that it?"
- Hank confirms by saying," You got it!"

Step 7 Person A asks for what he or she wants to resolve the issue or problem.

- Person A presents a plan for resolution and says, "I would like to (insert suggestion here) for us to resolve this problem."
- Be clear and specific about the suggested solution.

Example: Hank presents a solution to the problem.
Hanks says, "I would like us to agree that neither one of us will be on our devices when we are hanging out together, unless we have discussed and agreed to an exception."

Step 8 Person B clarifies and responds to what person A has requested.

- Clarify what person A is asking, and if you're in agreement, say, "Yes, I am willing to do that."
- If person B does not agree with the request, he or she asks for an opportunity to negotiate a different solution.

Example: Sonya agrees to the request.

- Sonya says," That is fair, and if you or I need to be on a device, we will check in with each other first."

Step 9 Person A and person B acknowledge their agreement.

- Together person A and person B develop a plan for implementation.

Example: Hank and Sonya agree that their phones will be off when they are hanging out together unless they both agree to an exception.

Step 10 Express appreciation for your Center-Stage Communication

- Person A says, "Thank you for listening to me and participating with me in Center-Stage Communication."

- Person B says, "Thank you for sharing this with me. This has been a wonderful way to present and resolve our issues."

Example: Hank and Sonya appreciate their Center-Stage Communication

- Hank says, "I know this was hard for us to discuss, and I really appreciate your willingness to listen fully and use Center-Stage Communication."
- Sonya responds, "I never want you to feel unimportant and am grateful that you shared your concerns."

Center-Stage Communication might trigger an issue or problem for person B. It is important to complete person A's Center-Stage Communication steps before moving into person B's first step.

Practice Center-Stage Communication, on some issues that are rated 1 to 3 in intensity to become comfortable with the technique before using it on issues rated as 5. Some issues are more difficult than others and will be more emotionally charged.

Lesson: Review and practice the following quick reference for Center-Stage Communication:

1. Recognize your issue.
2. Ask for Center-Stage Communication.
3. Agree to Center-Stage Communication.
4. Share your problem or issue.
5. Summarize what you heard.
6. Confirm and clarify.
7. Ask for what you want and propose a solution.
8. Respond to the request for a solution.
9. Both acknowledge agreement.
10. Appreciate and complete.

24. Reset the Moment

We are all perfectly imperfect and make mistakes. Sometimes mistakes require using a particular tool, such as Center-Stage Communication. Other times, mistakes only need a quick reset.

These are times when the issue is important but not significant. Critical issues need to be acknowledged and managed. Left unattended, these critical issues can become more significant and emotionally charged.

There are three highly effective practices to Reset the Moment by recognizing and quickly resolving hurt.

The three practices to Reset the Moment are the following:

1. Oops and Ouch
2. Do-Over
3. Take Five

1. Oops and Ouch

The first Reset the Moment practice is Oops and Ouch. When you notice that you have made a mistake by saying or doing something that might have hurt your partner, say, "Oops." Saying "Oops" is a simple way to stop, recognize your mistake, and reset the moment. The following are examples of using Oops and Ouch:

> "Oops. I'm sorry I ignored you when I came home. That was unkind. I would like to reset the moment. Is that okay with you?"

Saying "Oops" allows you to recognize your mistake and take responsibility. This simple tool helps you build and maintain a loving connection.

When you feel hurt by something your partner has done or said and your partner has not used "Oops," you can stop, recognize the hurt, and reset the moment by saying, "Ouch."

"Ouch. I feel ignored. I would like to stop and reset the moment with a do-over."

The use of Oops and Ouch helps you recognize a negative interaction, and this tool can be followed by a request for a Do-Over.

2. Do-Over

The second Reset the Moment practice is a Do-Over. A Do-Over starts with a request to stop and start again. The following is an example of a Do-Over:

> Sandy had an incredibly stressful day, and when she got home, she felt exhausted and irritable. She ignored Ryan when he got up to give her a hug. She shrugged off his hug and went to the bedroom to change.
>
> As she changed her clothes, she realized she had been rude and unkind to Ryan. When she came out of the bedroom, she apologized to Ryan and asked for a Do-Over.
>
> He smiled and said, "Sure."
>
> She went back to the front door, came in again, and, with a smile, said, "Hi, Ryan! I'm so glad to be home and to see you! How was your day?"
>
> Ryan hugged her and said, "I'm so glad you're here. My day was great. We can catch up at dinner."

The Do-Over is a light-hearted way for either partner to interrupt a negative moment and create a more positive connection.

3. Take Five

The third Reset the Moment practice is to Take Five. Taking five is like an adult time-out. It helps you reset and get back in control. You use the time and space to intentionally regain composure and get rebalanced. Focus on calming yourself rather than continuing to recycle negative thoughts. It is a time to stop feeding yourself the same negative thoughts and feelings that got you upset in the first place.

Steps to Take Five:

1. Announce that you need to Take Five.

   "I need to take five to get rebalanced."

2. Set a time limit.

   "I will be back in five minutes."

3. The partner who Takes Five returns and takes responsibility to reengage.

   "I'm ready to finish our conversation."

By using these steps, you physically remove yourself from the intensity of the moment. This enables you to examine your thoughts and feelings so you can reengage with your partner with greater clarity and composure.

While one partner is taking a time-out, it is helpful for the other partner to use the time to manage thoughts and feelings to get rebalanced as well.

Lesson: Use the Reset the Moment practices when you feel emotionally charged.

25. Heal the Hurts in Your Relationship

In a Mindful Loving relationship, the ability to make heartfelt apologies and forgive hurts is a significant marker of the strength of the relationship. In a Mindful Loving relationship, neither partner intends to cause hurt to the other partner, yet hurt occurs. It is inevitable that you will each experience hurt. Authentic loving means you will experience a depth and breadth of emotions from joy and exhilaration to pain and hurt. Pain is a natural result of being human, loving, and being vulnerable.

Pain is a catalyst for healing. Healing enables you to reconnect and grow stronger. When there is hurt in the relationship, both partners must participate in the healing process.

Apologizing, making amends, forgiving, and letting go are some of the most difficult practices partners encounter. When hurts are not healed, the failure to heal is often a result of an ineffective or incomplete apology and the lack of forgiveness.

Four practices to Heal the Hurts in Your Relationship are as follows:

1. Apologize.
2. Make amends.
3. Forgive.
4. Let go.

1. Apologize

Effective and complete apologies build trust and reconnection. Apologizing is a process that starts when you express remorse by saying, "I'm sorry" or "I apologize." Owning your behavior by admitting a mistake enables you to take responsibility. Putting yourself in your partner's shoes enables you to understand how your behavior hurt your partner. It requires self-awareness and a degree of vulnerability that includes humility and courage.

The practice of apologizing increases empathy, compassion, and understanding. When you apologize, you restore your partner's dignity and your own self-respect. At times, the simplicity and power of a heartfelt apology are enough to heal the hurt. Consider the following example:

> "I'm sorry I stayed on my phone and was insensitive when you were talking about your problems at work. I am going to turn off my phone now and would like to do a Do Over."

2. Make Amends

The second practice for this tool, Heal the Hurts in Your Relationship, is a practice that restores your own integrity when the hurt is deep and repeated.

Making amends is a practice wherein you move beyond your words of apology into action. Your commitment to a change in behavior becomes the living expression of your apology. This part of the healing process starts with you offering a way to make up for your mistake. It also includes asking your partner, "What do you need or want to help you heal?" Below is an example:

> "I'm sorry I was looking at porn on my computer. I know that hurts you. I am committed to changing this behavior. I will place controls on my computer that inhibit access to these sites, and I will give you my password.
> Is there anything else I can do to repair and rebuild your trust?"

3. Forgive

The third practice for healing hurts in your relationship is to forgive. Forgiving is an intentional decision to release feelings of resentment and hurt. When you make a mistake and hurt your partner, it is just as important for you to forgive yourself as it is to ask your partner for forgiveness. Forgiving is not a sign of weakness; it is a sign of strength. Forgiving is a practice for both partners and takes time to come to full resolution. Resolution for the offender might come with apologizing and making amends. The resolution for the partner who was hurt might take more time when the hurt is traumatic or touches a trauma wound from the past.

Forgiveness does not mean forgetting, condoning, or glossing over the offensive behavior. It does mean recognizing, validating, and expressing the hurt. Consider the following statement:

> "I know now how much my behavior hurt you. Will you forgive me? I am upset with myself for hurting you, and I know it is important for me to forgive myself and grow from this experience."

As a result of forgiving, each partner accepts the healing experience and can let go of the hurt to grow and reconnect.

4. Let Go

The fourth practice for healing the hurts in your relationship is to let go. Letting go releases you and your partner from the burden of carrying the pain into the future. Pain you hold on to can become like an old scar that begins to define you.

Letting go is a conscious choice to let go of the hurt and live in the moment. Letting go is about caring, being human, and making the most out of a mistake. When you stop retelling the story of the pain, letting go becomes more important than the hurt itself. Letting go allows you to regain peace, empowerment, and trust.

Lesson: Use these practices to Heal the Hurts in Your Relationship and move forward with greater passion and purpose.

26. Ask for What You Want and Say What You Don't Want

Ask for What You Want

Some people believe that asking for what they want in a relationship is selfish or being self-centered. The truth is, knowing and asking for what you want is one of the most honest, healthy, and loving practices you can do for both yourself and your partner.

Another common belief is "If you really love me, you'll know what I want or need!" This belief sets you and your partner up for unrealistic expectations in your relationship. It leads to mind reading, guessing, or making assumptions.

Asking your partner a particular question might provide information about your own wants and needs. For example, "Are you hungry?" might mean several things:

> You are hungry and want to know if your partner wants to eat.
> You want to go out to eat.
> You want your partner to prepare a meal.

An effective practice to Ask for What You Want is to answer your own question first. This practice helps you be clear and honest about your own wants and needs.

Steps to Answer Your Own Question First

1. Before asking your partner the question, "Are you hungry?" answer your own question first.
   "Am I hungry?"
2. Reflect on what you really want.
   "Hmm, I want to go out to dinner."
3. Be specific and communicate what you want.
   "I am hungry, and I would like to go out for Italian. Are you up for going out for Italian tonight?"

When you ask for what you want, you take responsibility for yourself instead of expecting your partner to take responsibility. You are the expert about your own wants and needs. By asking for what you want, you take responsibility and release your partner from the pressure of making assumptions or mindreading.

Say What You Don't Want

It is equally important to recognize what you don't want. You have the right to say, "No, thank you," to what you don't want. It is important that both partners recognize that no means no. Some of the things you don't want might include having sex, going out, entertaining, or taking a trip. Saying no is a necessary part of practicing self-care and setting healthy boundaries. Saying no is about being honest and respecting your own needs and wants. It is equally as important as saying yes in your Mindful Loving relationship.

An effective practice to Say What You Don't Want is to use a Permissible No. This practice helps you take responsibility for yourself and recognize your partner's request and vulnerability. It also helps you practice negotiation and resolution skills.

Steps for Using the Permissible No

1. Hear and acknowledge your partner's request.
   "So, you want to have sex, right?"
2. Reflect on your own wants and needs as they relate to the request.
   "I am really enjoying this moment."
3. Use the Permissible No and be honest with your partner about what you want and don't want.
   "I am really tired and preoccupied, and as much as I love your invitation, it's just not a good time for me right now."
4. Suggest an alternative.
   "How about continuing this tomorrow after work?"
5. Negotiate and agree on an alternative.
   "I appreciate your understanding and hope you are not too disappointed about tonight. I am glad we have agreed to pick up where we left off tomorrow night."

The Permissible No helps each partner honor wants and needs without guilt or feelings of rejection. Using these practices creates deeper understanding and acceptance.

Lesson: Practice asking for what you want by using the practice of answering your own question first. Practice saying what you don't want and use the Permissible No.

27. Practice Effective Negotiation

When partners are not in alignment with each other and have different wants and needs, they often fall into conflict that shows up in one of three ways.

1. The conflict explodes into a destructive fight.

   Often, the destructive fight is about the same old recycled problems and leaves each partner feeling hurt, angry, and stuck. The conflict stays unresolved.

2. The partners avoid dealing with the conflict.

   Some partners avoid dealing with differences in their wants and needs. One partner might be conflict avoidant which leaves the other partner frustrated. This results in unmet needs and a continual lack of resolution.

3. The partners Practice Effective Negotiation.

   Negotiation is a practice that results in compromise and agreement. This tool utilizes the Basics of Mindful Loving which are Loving Communication, and Understanding & Respecting Differences.

Negotiation is a practice that acknowledges and resolves differences.

Important steps in effective negotiation include the following:

1. Share what you want and don't want.

   Start by reflecting and acknowledging your own wants and needs as well as what you don't want. Use "I" Messages to share your feelings with your partner.

2. Listen to what your partner wants and doesn't want.

   This step helps you Listen from the Heart to Understand your partner's needs and wants without judgment or distraction.

3. Each partner rates the importance of his or her position

   This step enables each partner to recognize and rate the strength of his or her wants and needs.

   Use a scale from 1 to 5 as follows:
   1. Least important
   2. Mildly important
   3. Moderately important
   4. Very important
   5. Most important

   This rating system provides a framework for negotiation and resolution. Using this rating system helps you understand the level of passion and attachment, you each have to your own wants and needs. When one partner's number is at a 4 or 5 and the other partner's rating is lower, the negotiation is easier. Resolution leans toward the partner with the higher number. When both partners share a higher rating of a 4 or 5, the situation requires greater attention and effective negotiation.

4. Create acceptable solutions.

   By brainstorming, each partner contributes two to three viable solutions to the problem without critiquing the suggestions. Effective negotiation involves exploring the benefits and limitations of each suggestion.

5. Reach compromise and agreement.

   Sometimes completing steps 1 through 4 is enough to reach a mutually agreed upon solution. Other times, when there is a stalemate, a compromise is necessary.

   A compromise occurs when partners make concessions and accept something that is different or less than what they originally wanted. It involves considering the wishes of each partner and then adjusting a solution that both partners accept. The result of a compromise is mutually beneficial and creates resolution.

Agreements are more than words; they require action. Agreements mandate that you accept the solution and behave in different ways that help prevent the recycling of the same old conflict.

Lesson: Practice the steps for effective negotiation.

28. Practice Acceptance of Each Other's Differences

This tool, Practice Acceptance of Each Other's Differences is the living expression of the second basic component of Mindful Loving which is Understanding & Respecting Differences. The following three practices help you implement this tool:

1. Practice the Golden Rule of Mindful Loving.
2. Be each other's Go-To Person.
3. Manage Differences with Love and Respect.

1. Practice the Golden Rule of Mindful Loving

The Golden Rule of Mindful Loving says, "Love your partner the way your partner wants to be loved."

Have a conversation about your practice of the Golden Rule of Mindful Loving, and use the following as guidelines:

- Make a list of ways you each want to be loved.
- Make a list of ways you each show love to your partner.
- Have fun sharing and reviewing your lists.
- From your sharing, create a master list that represents how you each can effectively follow the Golden Rule of Mindful Loving.

As you move through the Cycles of Mindful Loving, your needs and wants change and grow. By using this tool, you not only stay in touch with changes in yourself, you also stay in touch with changes in your partner. This practice creates a safe place in your Mindful Loving relationship that sustains the foundation of your passion and purpose.

2. Be Each Other's Go-To Person

In a Mindful Loving relationship, each partner is the one person, above all others, with whom the other partner shares his or her most meaningful and intimate experiences.

Have a conversation about being each other's Go-To Person and use the following as guidelines:

- Share stories about ways your partner has acted as your Go-To Person.
- Identify the behaviors that contributed to you feeling supported.
- Share times when you and your partner championed and supported each other.
- Commit to those unique practices to ensure you maintain being each other's Go-To Person.

3. Manage Differences with Love and Respect

Managing differences in your Mindful Loving is a practice that requires ongoing attention. Some of our key differences and similarities are experienced in the following areas: religion and spirituality, culture and lifestyle, personality and age, and brain and sexuality.

Have a conversation about your differences and similarities in each of these areas, and use the following guidelines:

- Recognize and identify differences and similarities.
- Talk about how you each show love and respect as you manage those differences.
- Chose a practice that helps you manage one of your differences.

Lesson: Practice acceptance of differences daily.

29. Manage Communication Differences

It is important to understand the different ways in which you process and express information. Once you understand these differences, it is easier to accept them and learn ways to manage them. People process and express information on a continuum of communication styles and often use a combination of styles in their conversations.

Three-Step Process to Manage Communication Differences

1. Each of you starts by identifying your own communication style for processing and expressing information.

2. Share your styles with each other.

3. Discuss ways you can manage your communication style differences.

To complete step 1, consider the following communication styles for processing and expressing information. Use this information to identify your own communication styles.

> **Processing Information:** Processing information is how you access data, learn something new, make a decision, share information, or solve a problem. Some communication styles in processing information include:
> - internal processing and external processing;
> - analytical processing and creative processing;
> - problem-solving processing and sharing-information processing;
> - focus-on-detail processing and focus-on-big-picture processing;
> - visual, auditory, and experiential processing;
>
> **Expressing Information:** Expressing information is how you express your thoughts and feelings based on your own unique

style of communication. Some communication styles in expressing information include:

- internal expressing and external expressing;
- analytical expressing and creative expressing;
- problem-solving expressing and sharing-information expressing;
- focus-on-detail expressing and focus-on-big-picture expressing;
- visual, auditory, and experiential expressing;

To complete step 2, share your communication style with your partner. The following are some examples to complete step 2:

Internal Processing and External Processing

Bob recognizes that he uses internal processing. This means he begins to process information internally in his head.

Carol recognizes that she uses external processing. This means she starts talking aloud as she thinks about information.

Internal Expressing and External Expressing

Bob recognizes that he uses internal expressing. He expresses his thoughts as a decision without sharing the details of his internal processing.

Carol recognizes that she uses external expressing. She expresses all the thoughts and details that come into her head.

Analytical Processing and Creative Processing

Kim recognizes she uses analytical processing. She uses concrete and logical data to process information.

Barbara recognizes she uses creative processing. She uses intuition and feelings to process information.

Analytical Expressing and Creative Expressing

Kim uses analytical expressing and communicates in clear, succinct ways.

Barbara uses creative expressing and communicates with expanded stories and feelings.

Problem-Solving Processing and Sharing-Information Processing

Joe recognizes he uses problem-solving processing. He listens to collect data to solve a problem.

Joan recognizes she uses sharing-information processing. She uses data to explain and share a story.

Problem-Solving Expressing and Sharing-Information Expressing

Joe uses problem-solving expressing. He primarily responds with a suggestion, solution, or question, even when there is no stated problem.

Joan uses sharing-information expressing. She weaves a story around information with different intentions including
- a story about events in her day:
- a story about events in her day and a problem she encountered:
- a story about events in her day and a problem she encountered that needs to be solved.

Focus-on-Details Processing and Focus-on-Big-Picture Processing

Bill recognizes he uses focus-on-details processing. He zooms in on the causes and details of the information.

Emily recognizes she uses focus-on-big-picture processing. She focuses on a broader perspective with consideration for the effect of the situation.

Focus-on-Details Expressing and Focus-on-Big-Picture Expressing

Bill uses focus-on-details expressing. He focuses on the specifics and details of the conversation. His words are brief and succinct.

Emily uses focus-on-big-picture expressing. She uses many words to express her experience with the situation. Her words are descriptive and express the broader picture of the conversation.

Visual Processing, Auditory Processing, and Experiential Processing

David recognizes he uses visual processing. He primarily relies on what he sees to process data.

Molly recognizes she uses auditory processing. She relies primarily on what she hears.

Ari recognizes she uses experiential processing. She primarily relies on her personal experience when processing information.

Visual Expressing, Auditory Expressing, and Experiential Expressing

David uses visual expressing. To express himself, he uses language like the following: "I see what you mean."

Molly uses auditory expressing. She uses language like the following: "I hear what you are saying."

Ari uses experiential expressing. She uses language like the following: "In my experience..."

To complete step 3, discuss ways to manage your communication style differences.

Internal and External Processing and Expressing

After sharing their communication style differences, Bob and Carol discuss ways to manage their differences. Bob learns to express his thoughts and details of his internal processing aloud. Carol learns to think about the details internally and only shares the most significant details of her processing aloud.

Analytical and Creative Processing and Expressing

After sharing their communication styles, Kim and Barbara have a conversation about ways to manage their differences. Kim learns to acknowledge and accept the value of creative and intuitive ideas. This results in a more expansive conversation.

Barbara learns to accept and integrate the value of logical data. This results in a more focused and concise conversation.

Problem-Solving and Sharing-Information Processing and Expressing

After identifying and sharing their communication differences, Joe and Joan discuss ways to manage those differences. Joe learns to listen to understand and asks before offering solutions.

Joan learns to identify the intention of her sharing information and lets her partner know what she needs:
- to be heard,
- to be supported,
- and to have help solving a problem.

Focus-on-Details and Focus-on-Big-Picture Processing and Expressing

After sharing their communication style differences, Bill and Emily discuss ways to manage those differences. Bill learns to be patient as he listens to Emily's broader perspective. He practices withholding his response until she has fully completed her part of the conversation.

Emily learns to accept Bill's need for details and asks questions about the details that help both gain mutual understanding of the information.

Visual, Auditory, and Experiential Processing and Expressing

After identifying their communication-style differences, David, Molly and Ari share their communication styles with their partners and discuss ways to manage the differences. David learns to ask questions such as, "What does that look like?", to understand his partner's auditory or experiential expressing.

Molly learns to ask questions such as, "Help me understand; tell me more", to understand her partner's visual or experiential expressing.

Ari learns to ask for examples or stories to understand her partner's visual or auditory expressing.

Lesson: Review and practice the 3-step process to Manage Your Communication Differences.

30. Use Technology Wisely

Using technology wisely means knowing when and how to use it in your Mindful Loving relationship. The world of digital connection and technology has become a primary medium for human interaction. Many partners spend an average of twelve hours a day in front of a screen, which directly impacts the quality of their communication and human connection.

There are both advantages and disadvantages to the use of technology.

One of the greatest advantages of technology is that it provides partners with multiple ways to communicate and maintain connection. Technological devices and social media offer a wide range of communication options. When used wisely, these devices and social media help partners enhance human connection with short love texts, heartfelt apologies, photos to capture the moment, and the coordination of calendars. Many couples use computers and smartphones to get and share educational information that strengthens their relationship. In Mindful Loving relationships, the use of technology is intentional, not compulsive.

One of the greatest disadvantages of technology is the possibility of digital connection becoming more important than human connection. If you are moving your thumbs more than your mouth, you know you have a digital problem. An example of this problem is when partners are together and choose to be on their devices instead of connecting with each other. This can happen when you are at dinner, in the car, or on the couch together.

Another disadvantage of digital connection is the tendency for partners to send hurtful, angry, or abusive texts, communicating things they would never say in person. This allows impulsive, instant, and irresponsible communication. Digital connections have other disadvantages, including the potential for having secret emotional and sexual relationships, spying on each other, and sharing inappropriate private and intimate information with others known and unknown.

The ding of a text can stimulate the pleasure center of the brain and hijack your attention from being present with your partner. The constant search for instant gratification comes at the cost of true connection.

Have you ever felt frustrated when you are talking with your partner and the notification ding distracts your partner from the conversation? Some partners experience a compulsion to immediately check the notification and become disengaged from the conversation.

The tool, Use Technology Wisely, requires you to talk about the effect of technology in your Mindful Loving relationship. Talk about when and how to use technology to maintain your healthy, Mindful Loving relationship and create your own guidelines.

Some examples of guidelines include the following:

1. Decide when, where, and for how long it is okay to use technology.

   Ask questions like the following:

   > "Is it okay to use our devices while we are in bed together, on a date, watching TV together, or out with friends or family?"
   > "When is it not okay to use our devices?"

2. Decide on technology-free times and places.

   - Schedule digital-free zones and times.
   - Help each other remember to honor digital-free times and zones.
   - Use digital-free times for Big Talk conversations, dates, or sex.

3. Decide about privacy for devices.

   Ask yourselves questions like the following:

   > "Do we want to share our passwords with each other?"

"Is it okay to check each other's devices with or without permission?"

If the answer is "yes," clarify when and for what reasons.
If the answer is "no," share the reason.

4. Decide on the use and sharing of social media accounts.

Ask yourselves questions like the following:

"Can we share a Facebook account, or should we have separate accounts?"
"Should we close our social media accounts?"
"What are the pros and cons of using our social media accounts?"

5. Decide how and when to use texts.

Ask yourselves questions like the following:

"What is appropriate content for our texting, information, and sharing?"
"What is our expectation for how soon we respond?"
"Are we willing to commit to no fighting or sending hurtful communications via texts?"

Every day holds an infinite array of opportunities to live a purposeful life. The use of technology can present a challenge for those who are constantly caressing mobile phones, curating their social media profiles, and waiting for the next digital signal to give them purpose.

Finding your true purpose and leading a purposeful life does not mean abandoning the digital world. It simply means you must recognize that there is a huge divide between digital connections and deep and meaningful human connections.

As you examine the road ahead in a world filled with artificial intelligence, machine learning, and robotics, it is imperative that you never forget who you are as a human being. You were born to live, laugh, love, and to connect.

Lesson: Use Technology Wisely and create a balance between digital and human connection.

31. Be a Lifelong Student of Mindful Loving

Mindful Loving is a lifelong experience and practice. This tool is about your commitment to engaging in on going learning opportunities. There are several ways to engage in learning opportunities.

Here are some examples:

1. Talk about what you each learned about relationships from your family of origin.

   Some questions to consider are as follows:
   "In what ways do I act like my mother or father?"
   "What are the values I learned from the modeling in my home?"
   "What are the behaviors I do and don't want to repeat in my Mindful Loving relationship?"
   "How do I want to be in my own Mindful Loving relationship?"

2. Read books, articles, and blogs; listen to podcasts; and watch TED Talks and YouTube videos about relationships.

3. Participate in educational workshops, seminars, retreats and church or professional support groups for couples.

4. Observe other couples in your family and social circles.

   Ask yourself,
   "What do I like or not like about what I observed? What can I do to be more or less like what I witnessed?"

5. Observe couples in movies, on TV, or in educational videos, and assess and share your impressions.

   Ask yourself the following questions:

"What did I like most about the way the partners connected with each other?"

"What did we learn from how the characters interacted?"

"What can we learn about ourselves and our own relationship from the characters in the media?"

Keep in mind that characters in the media are not real, and when observing relationships in your family or social circle you are only seeing a part of the whole picture.

Lesson: Stay open to learning new things about yourself, your partner, and your relationship.

32. Create Spiritual Connections

When you have a spiritual practice at the center of your Mindful Loving relationship, you create a foundation of love, passion, purpose, and joy. A spiritual connection is a soul connection based on beliefs and practices that reflect living with purpose from your highest and best selves.

Many couples find this connection through their religious communities. They participate in enrichment programs, such as couples' Bible study programs, marriage encounters, retreats, workshops, or relationship seminars.

Other couples design their spiritual connections through their own unique practices. These couples create spiritual connections through meditating, reading, and creating sacred time for spiritual connection at home or in nature.

Here are some ways you can enhance the spiritual connection in your Mindful Loving relationship:

- Explore your own spiritual practices.
- Identify ways you make spiritual connections in your own life.
- Share what you each value in your spiritual practices.
- Share the practices that will enrich your spiritual connection.
- Plan to add one or two practices into your Mindful Loving relationship.

Lesson: Share your spirituality by making a daily practice of praying, meditating, reading, or writing.

33. Create a Mindful Loving Relationship Vision Statement

A Mindful Loving Relationship Vision Statement is a statement that reflects your core values and your relationship vision. It is a statement that nurtures your passion and purpose. Your vision statement is dynamic and inspiring. It helps you create goals that reflect the two basic components of Mindful Loving: Loving Communication and Understanding & Respecting Differences. It serves as a guide through the Cycles of Mindful Loving relationships.

Here are some guidelines to help you create your Mindful Loving Relationship Vision Statement:

1. Sit together to review any vows or commitment statements you have made in the past.

2. Make a list of words and concepts that represent your core values and your relationship vision and purpose. Some common core values include the following:

   - love

   - honesty

   - respect

   - trust

   - vulnerability

   - care

   - openness

   - integrity

   - accountability

- discipline

Your relationship vision and purpose answers such questions like the following:

> "What are our hopes and dreams for our Mindful Loving relationship?"

> "What initially drew us together?"

> "What keeps us together now?"

> "What are our goals and promises for our Mindful Loving relationship?"

3. Create your statement, and use the following:

- Make it positive.

- Make it present.

- Make it personal

- Make it powerful.

- Make it align with your Mindful Loving vision.

Some examples of a Mindful Loving Relationship Vision Statement include the following:

- We are loving partners living our lives with passion, purpose, and joy.

- We are committed to be our best selves and to help each other grow.

- We communicate openly and honestly.

- We create our dreams and make them happen.

- We understand, respect, and accept our differences.

Lesson: Create Your Mindful Loving Relationship Vision Statement and live it with passion and purpose.

34. Create and Use Goals to Fulfill Your Mindful Loving Vision

Keep your Mindful Loving relationship vision alive by creating goals that enable you to live according to your vision statement. Goals are practical action items that turn your vision into a reality.

Goals are tools to help you stay focused in a positive direction. Reviewing and evaluating goals on a monthly basis helps you recognize your successes and accomplishments and alerts you to areas that need more work and attention. The review and evaluation practices help you update and reset goals for the next month. This keeps you accountable and focused on fulfilling your Mindful Loving vision.

We encourage you to think about your goals in the following way:

G	Great
O	Opportunity to
A	Align with
L	Lifelong loving
S	Success

The three important goal-setting components are as follows:

- Create SMART goals.
- Review and evaluate your goals.
- Update and reset your goals.

These three components create the structure that enables you to live according to your Mindful Loving Relationship vision statement.

Create Smart Goals

You can create SMART goals by using the following:

S   Specific
M   Measurable
A   Attainable
R   Relevant
T   Time-based

Successful goals follow the SMART goal format. For example, if you and your partner want to increase intimacy in your relationship, the goal "Create greater intimacy" is not a SMART goal. The SMART goal for greater intimacy would be "Take five or more minutes for Big-Talk conversations every day to increase our intimate connections."

Big-Talk conversations include sharing what you think and how you feel about your daily experiences. These conversations also allow you to share your deeper emotional experiences, which helps you to maintain intimacy.

Here are some areas and examples to consider for SMART goal setting:

- Mindful Loving Practices
  SMART Goal: Select one Mindful Loving relationship tool each week to practice together.

- Managing Finances
  SMART Goal: Create and implement a budget that reduces our debt by 5 percent by the end of the year.

- Parenting Our Children
  SMART Goal: Create an agenda and plan a weekly family meeting to discuss family activities and responsibilities and have Big-Talk conversations about family experiences.

- Commitment to Having Fun Together
  SMART Goal: Plan, coordinate, and schedule one or more fun activities for yourselves every month.

- Home Management
  SMART Goal: Create a home-management chore list (laundry, bill paying, yard work, cooking, cleaning, grocery shopping, etc.). Identify the partner responsible for each chore and when and how the chore will be completed.

- Individual and Relationship Care:
  SMART Goal: Create a weekly or monthly self-care plan, and share it. Together create a relationship care plan that ensures time for weekly meaningful connection and intimacy.

Review and Evaluate Goals

To ensure the successful fulfillment of your Mindful Loving Relationship visions statement, it is important to review and evaluate your goals on a regular basis.

The best way to conduct this review is to schedule thirty minutes or more of uninterrupted time to meet every month to review and evaluate progress toward your goals. Some people choose the same day and time every month and schedule the evaluations for the year.

Review your progress by scoring each of your goals using a scale of 0-100 percent for completion. A 100 percent score on a goal indicates that you have been successful this month in meeting that goal. Once you reach 100 percent, you may choose to continue to focus on that goal, or you might set a new goal for that area. A score of 80 percent or less indicates a goal that needs greater attention or you might need to restructure the goal into smaller and more specific goals.

Evaluate your progress by discussing your accomplishments and disappointments. Think about what you did to reach the accomplishments. Those actions are the practices that will lead you to continued success.

Discuss your disappointments, and create new practices that will help you overcome the disappointments and move you toward greater success.

Update and Reset Goals

This part of the goal-setting process helps you maintain progress in meeting your SMART goals. Updating means using the information from the review and evaluation to create the next month's goals.

You may continue to use the same goal every month to ensure that it becomes a new habit. You reset by creating new goals that align with your Mindful Loving relationship vision statement.

Lesson: Create five or more SMART goals, and schedule review dates on the calendar.

35. Get Professional Help When Needed

We all need help at times. No one is immune from having difficulties in a relationship. It is a sign of strength to be able to ask for help when you need it. Reading a book like this and using the Practical Tools can be an immensely helpful first step.

Relationship coaching or couples counseling can provide guidance and help to heal and strengthen your relationship. If you have tried to use self-help tools and they are not working for you; you have suffered a traumatic event, such as infidelity; you are considering ending the relationship; or you just need some outside perspective, don't hesitate to reach out for professional help.

Be proactive in seeking professional help when needed. It can be one of the best gifts you give yourself and each other.

Lesson: Be proactive and ask for help when needed.

Using the Practical Tools for Mindful Loving

These Practical Tools for Mindful Loving offer skills and practices that you can learn and develop. Be patient with yourself; it takes time and practice to make new skills your own. Using the Practical Tools will help you make your relationship more passionate and purposeful.

Choosing the appropriate tools for your own Mindful Loving relationship makes the work easier and more effective. You will need diverse types of tools for your relationship toolbox. Most importantly, use the tools regularly to enhance your Mindful Loving relationship.

Final Thoughts

We all have a desire for connection, acceptance, and love. Mindful Loving is a choice partners make to help fulfill this desire. It takes daily commitment to practice living and loving more fully. When we live and love more fully, we live with greater passion and purpose.

Passion involves shared joys, exhilarations, and sexual and emotional connections, that radiate throughout our Mindful Loving relationship. Our passion comes from the core of who we are. Identifying and experiencing our own passion enables us to share that passion in our Mindful Loving relationships. This sharing passion generates passion between us and manifests in our relationships. Passion is the fuel that ignites and sustains love and connection throughout the Cycles of Mindful Loving.

Purpose is the reason we live the lives we live. Our purpose defines who we are and why we are driven to do what we do and love whom we love. Identifying and understanding our own purpose is necessary to develop the purpose for our Mindful Loving relationship. It is important to reassess our purpose as we journey through the Cycles of Mindful Loving. Defining our purpose stabilizes the present and sets the future of our Mindful Loving in motion.

This book is intended as our gift to you, and now it is the gift you give yourself. You give yourself this gift by using the information in this book. Start with the intention to enhance and enrich your relationship. Next, make a commitment to do the work that Mindful Loving requires. Then make the commitment to practice the basics of Mindful Loving and use the Practical Tools in order to create your own Mindful Loving relationship.

Every couple can create their own Mindful Loving relationship. It takes assessment, commitment, and practice to create and transform any relationship into a Mindful Loving relationship.

You are the author of your own Mindful Loving relationship story. The love from your Mindful Loving relationship cascades and spreads from you and touches the people around you. Your story is not only your story; it affects you, your partner, your family and friends, and the world around you. The power of Mindful Loving brings love, joy, and healing to you, others, and our world.

Resources

Books

Amen, Daniel. *Change Your Brain, Change Your Life*. New York: Harmony Press, 2015.

Amen, Daniel. *Love in the Brain: 12 Lessons to Enhance Your Love Life*. New York: Three Rivers Press, 2009.

Arylo, Christine. *Choosing ME before WE: Every Woman's Guide to Life and Love*. Novato, CA: New World Library, 2009.

Brown, Brené. *Braving the Wilderness: The Quest for True Belonging and the Courage to Stand Alone*. New York: Random House, 2017.

Brown, Brené. *Daring Greatly*. New York: Penguin Random House, 2012.

Brown, Brené. *The Gifts of Imperfection*. Center City, MN: Hazelden, 2010.

Calhoun, Adele. *Spiritual Disciplines Handbook: Practices That Transform Us*. Downers Grove, IL: IVP Books, 2015.

Carlson, Randy. *Starved for Affection*. Colorado Springs: Tyndale House, 2005.

Chapman, Gary. *The Five Love Languages: The Secret to Love That Lasts*. Chicago: Northfield Publishing, 2013.

Chopra, Deepak. *The Seven Spiritual Laws of Success*. New York: Amber-Allen Publishing, 1994.

Chopra, Deepak. *The Spontaneous Fulfillment of Desire*. New York: Random House, 2003.

Davis, Megan, and Kathleen Todd. *I'm in Charge: A Parenting Strategy to Help You Raise Happy and Cooperative Children*. Tempe, AZ: Lulu Press, 2014.

Davis, Megan, and Kathleen Todd. *The Little Book of Parenting Tools.* Tempe, AZ: Lulu Press, 2014.

DeAngelis, Barbara. *Real Moments.* New York: Dell Publishing, 1994.

Ditzler, Jinny. *Your Best Year Yet!* New York: Warner Books, 1994.

Earle, Marcus, Ralph Earle, and Kevin Osborn. *Sex Addiction and Case Management.* Levittown, PA: Brunner/Mazel, 1995.

Eden, Donna and David Feinstein. *Energies of Love: Keys to a Fulfilling Partnership.* New York: Penguin Random House, 2016.

Gawande, Atul. *Being Mortal: Medicine and What Matters in the End.* New York: Metropolitan Books, 2014.

Gottman, John, Julie Schwartz Gottman, Douglas Abrams, and Rachel Abrams. *The Man's Guide to Women.* New York: Simon and Schuster, 2016.

Gottman, John, and Nan Silver. *What Makes Love Last? How to Build Trust and Avoid Betrayal.* New York: Harmony Books, 2015.

Gray, John. *Men Are from Mars, Women Are from Venus.* New York: Harper Collins, 1992.

Hallowell, Edward, and Hallowell, Susan. *Married to Distraction: Restoring Intimacy and Strengthening Your Marriage in an Age of Interruption.* New York:

Random House, 2010.

Hendrix, Harville. *Getting the Love You Want.* New York: Holt and Company, 2008.

Hendricks, Gay, and Hendricks, Kathlyn *Conscious Loving: The Journey to Co-Commitment.* Westminster, MD: Bantam Books, 1992.

Henricks, Gay, and Hendricks, Kathlyn. *Conscious Loving Ever After.* New York: Hay House, 2015.

Johnson, Susan. *Hold Me Tight: Seven Conversations for a Lifetime of Love.* New York: Little, Brown, and Company, 2008.

Katie, Byron. *Loving What Is.* New York: Harmony Books, 2002.

Kirshenbaum, Mira. *I Love You, but I Don't Trust You: The Complete Guide to Restoring Trust in Your Relationship.* New York: Penguin Group, 2012.

Kusi, Marcus and Ashley. *Questions for Couples: 469 Thought-Provoking Conversation Starters for Connecting, Building Trust, and Rekindling Intimacy.* Archangel Link, 2017.

Loeher, Jim and Tony Schwartz. *The Power of Full Engagement.* New York: Free Press, 2003.

Martin, Dianne. *The Book of Intentions.* Hillsboro, OR: Beyond Words Publishing, 2002.

McKay, Matthew, and Patrick Fanning. *Couple Skills: Making Your Relationship Work.* Oakland, CA: New Harbinger Publications, 2006.

Mintz, Lauri. *Becoming Cliterate: Why Orgasm Equality Matters—and How to Get It.* New York: Harper Collins, 2018.

Nagoski, Emily. *Come as You Are.* New York: Simon and Schuster, 2015.

Perel, Esther. *Mating in Captivity: Unlocking Erotic Intelligence.* New York: HarperCollins, 2006.

Perel, Esther. *The State of Affairs: Rethinking Infidelity.* New York: HarperCollins, 2017.

Patterson, Kerry, Joseph Grenny, Ron McMillan, Al Switzler. *Crucial Conversations: Tools for Talking When the Stakes Are High.* New York: McGraw-Hill, 2002.

Richo, David. *How to Be an Adult in the Relationship: The Five Keys to Mindful Loving.* New York: Shambala Publications, 2002.

Richo, David. *When the Past Is Present: Healing the Emotional Wounds That Sabbotage Our Relationships.* New York: Shambala Publications, 2008.

Rosenthal, Neil. *Love, Sex, and Staying Warm: Creating a Vital Relationship.* Boulder, CO: Flagstaff Mountain Press, 2016.

Sanberg, Sheryl, and Adam Grant. *Option B: Facing Adversity, Building Resilience, and Finding Joy.* New York: Penguin Random House, 2017.

Sharbuno, Jeanne. *52 Ways to Live Success—from the Inside Out!* Sanford, FL: DC Press, 2002.

Siegel, Daniel. *The Mindful Brain.* New York: W. W. Norton and Company, 2007.

Tatkin, Stanley. *Wired for Love: How Understanding Your Partner's Brain Can Help You Defuse Conflicts and Spark Intimacy.* Oakland, CA: New Harbinger, 2011.

Welwood, John. *Perfect Love, Imperfect Relationship: Healing the Wound of the Heart.* Boston: Trumpeter, 2006.

Printed in the United States
By Bookmasters